Schedule Centered Planning

An Incremental Approach
for
Plan Driven Projects

Vincent McGevna, PMP

www.pmsuccess.com

ACKNOWLEDGEMENTS

To all the project managers who graciously allowed me to observe their mistakes so I could learn from theirs as well as my own; to the managers who forced me to be creative in dealing with unreasonable demands; to the users who taught me what quality means; and to all the project team members who did all of the hard work.

Specifically I would like to thank Oliver Gildersleeve for the many discussions that planted the concept of focusing on the schedule and making it the plan; Gary Breeding and Terence Newman for their fruitful discussions and their direct input and editorial assistance; and all of the PMI members from the myriad meetings and breakfasts which always provided fresh ideas and perspectives.

TABLE OF CONTENTS

Vincent McGevna

1 Introduction

The most important thing a project manager can do is to plan – a good project plan is the best way to assure the success of a project. Not only does this produce a blueprint for how the project should proceed, but, insights gained during planning allow the project manager to quickly and effectively deal with the inevitable unforeseen events.

Schedule Centered Planning is not a radically new approach to planning, but it is unique. Following the process produces plans that are iterative. That is the end product is developed incrementally. The process is also concurrent – all aspects of the plan are dealt with in a holistic manner – and it recognizes that a properly developed schedule must reflect all other aspects of the overall plan. Thus your schedule is the primary component of your plan.

Planning Context

Planning starts with a definition of the project or its scope. First and foremost are requirements, which might be in the form of a formal specification or they may just be a list of features. Along with the requirements you will likely need a concept of the final product. This might be a simple sketch or description, or it may be a carefully thought out architecture. Both the requirements and the concept must reference any external projects or products, such as a legacy system, that will have to be modified, or that might be impacted by the current project. For example, the end deliverable, or even an intermediate deliverable from this project might be used in some other project.

In addition, most organizations have carefully thought out development processes laying out how different products are to be developed. Included in the processes are deliverables that have to be developed and procedures that have to be followed. These will also have a major impact on your planning.

Together, the Project and Processes define the context in which you will develop your project plan.

Planning Elements

Elements in a typical project plan include:

A *Schedule*: this is the detailed timeline for the project which is used to predict the end date and key intermediate milestones.

A *Budget*: this captures all project costs, and may include the time frame in which expenditures are made. Resources are frequently the main contributor to the budget, and sometimes the only contributor.

The *Risk Plan*: major project risks are identified, quantified and dealt with to reduce or eliminate their impact on the project. Risks are identified and quantified during schedule and budget creation, and risk mitigation is addressed in the schedule. The schedule and budget might also contain contingency to further deal with risk.

The *Quality Plan*: largely driven by the development process, this lays out what must be done to assure a quality product. Quality activities are included in the schedule.

The *Procurement Plan*: when procured hardware or software are required, making sure they are available when needed is essential. Procurement is closely associated with the budget, and procurement activities must be captured in the schedule.

The schedule, budget and scope together constitute what is known as the triple constraint. If you change one of them, then the other two will change. Put another way, management can specify at most two of them. If the scope and budget are fixed then the project duration will be determined by the amount of work in the scope and the total number of resources to do that work.

There are other planning elements which are very important and drive the actual planning elements. First is the work breakdown structure or WBS. This breaks down the scope into more manageable pieces. For each piece there must be an estimate of the work and for some, an estimate of the cost. Resources must be identified and assigned to the work. Also, it's best for the resources who do the actual work to make the estimates, at least the final estimates.

Schedule Centered Planning Process

Figure 1.1 shows a simplified flow diagram of the Schedule Centered Planning Process, showing how the planning elements interrelate.

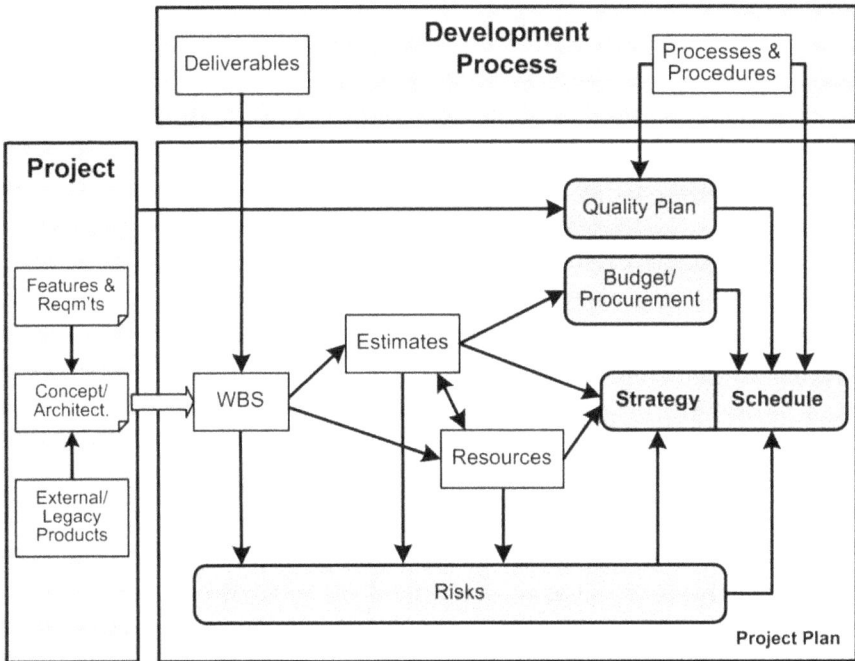

Figure 1.1. An Overview of the Schedule Centered Planning Process.

The project plan is driven by the *Project* definition, and the organization's development *Processes*. These will be discussed in the next chapter.

Note in the flow that the budget and procurement are combined into one plan. In my experience, the only time an actual budget is required is when there are major purchases. So these would be developed together.

Also, coupled with the schedule is a strategy. The strategy is the big picture view of the schedule – essentially the game plan where you lay out how to best bring about a successful project. The schedule then contains the necessary details of who does what when to execute the strategy.

Finally, all risk, quality and procurement activities must be captured in the schedule. In addition, major risks will drive your strategy and work or duration estimates in your schedule must reflect the risks associated with the deliverables.

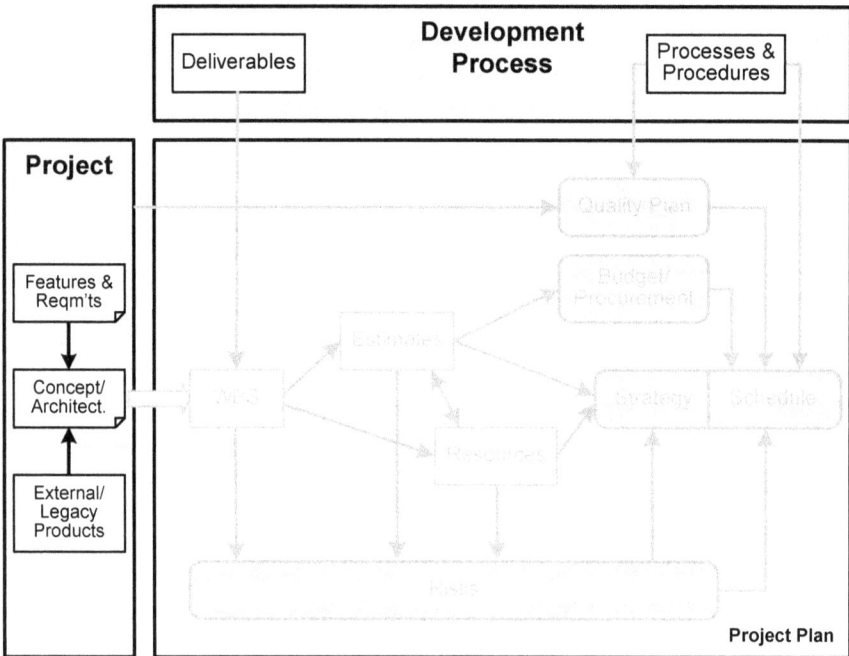

Development Process

Deliverables   Processes & Procedures

Project

Features & Reqm'ts

Concept/ Architect.

External/ Legacy Products

Quality Plan

Budget/ Procurement

Estimates

MRD   Strategy   Schedule

Resources

Risks

Project Plan

2 The Planning Context

Your project plan is based on what you must deliver, the project scope, and the process you must follow as you create it, your organization's development process. Before getting into the details of planning, we must consider these.

Project Definition

You can't start your project without a definition of what you have to do. This may be as simple as a list of features detailing what is expected. Or it may be in the form of a detailed requirements specification. Either way, there must be agreement up front on the total scope of the project. In addition, many projects require a concept or architecture which maps the requirements into the top level design of the final product. When needed, it is the basis for the WBS.

Generally, the project manager is not responsible for creating the requirements specification or the architecture. But the project manager should at least make sure that the requirements are complete and that they meet the needs of all who need to use them. While we will not go into how to create requirements, you should be aware that good requirements address:

- Need for the final product
- Functional requirements
- Operational Scenarios
- Non-functional requirements
- External products or projects (i.e. a legacy system)

Also, you should identify and record what's not in the project deliverable. Many stakeholders will not take "no" for an answer, and the only way to deal with them is to have a baselined document which clearly states what will and will not be included in the upcoming release.

Frequently planning and concept or architecture development are done in parallel. Here it's good to have regular informal conversations with those creating the architecture to gain understanding and insight both for creating the plan and for subsequently managing the development.

Development Process

The requirements and architecture address what is unique about your project; your organization's development process addresses what is repeatable across projects. It defines the deliverables that must be created and the processes and procedures that must be followed. Deliverables may include the Requirements and a number of different Design Documents. For example, if you're creating a printed circuit board, you will need a timing analysis and a thermal analysis.

Unfortunately, not all organizations have process documentation. Here you should look at past projects, and talk to the other project managers. What you need to identify is the process deliverables, who is responsible for each, and when it is produced in the development cycle.

When dealing with cross functional teams, it's useful to identify the deliverables for each major group within the organization's structure. For example, consider the development of a printed circuit board. The board is designed by an Electrical Engineer, but it also requires work by Mechanical and Software Engineers, and Board Test must set up the test system for production boards. Key deliverables from each group are listed in the table below. If you create a table like this for your organization it will make planning easier and you're less likely to overlook something.

Electrical	Mechanical	Software	Board Test
Functional Spec	Outline Drawing	Device Drivers:	Test Plans:
Block Diagram	Thermal Analysis	Specification	In-Circuit
Schematic		Design	Functional
Timing Analysis		Software	Boundary
Board layout		Test Plan	Scan
Bill of Materials		Test Software	Test Hardware
Etc.			Test Software

Table 2.1 Deliverables for a Printed Circuit Board.

While a table of deliverables is very useful to prevent omitting something important, it is even more useful to take these deliverables and lay out a generic schedule so you know where each fits into the cycle.

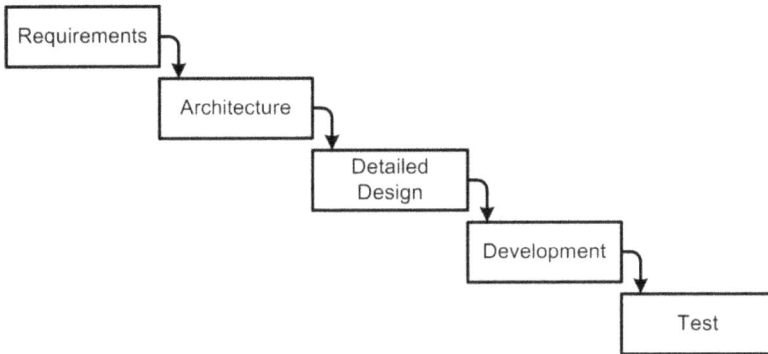

Figure 2.1 The Waterfall Development Process

Specific Development Processes

Many organizations follow a specific development process. For example, the waterfall process (Figure 2.1) is a sequential development process where each key deliverable is created and reviewed before starting work on the next deliverable.

The typical phases and corresponding reviews in a waterfall process are listed below:

Deliverable	Review
Requirements	Requirements Review
Architecture	Conceptual Design Review
Detailed Design	Detailed Design Review
Development	Test Readiness Review
Test	Acceptance Review

Because it is sequential and the reviews can be quite time consuming – to create the review material, to perform the reviews and then to update the documents – waterfall tends to be a slow development process.

 There are other processes that have evolved to resolve some of the deficiencies in waterfall. We'll take a cursory look at the two most popular alternatives: Phase Gate and Agile.

Phase Gate

Phase gate was developed to speed up the waterfall process, and is used quite a bit in new product development. As shown in Figure 2.2 (opposite) it appears to be similar to waterfall. However, rather than sequentially going through the deliverables, it specifies a sequence of phases, and the waterfall documents (Requirements, Architecture, etc.) , if required, are developed across a number of phases. Thus one can start before its predecessor is complete. (For example, architectural design will start when the key, top level requirements have been identified, but before the requirements document has been completed.) At the end of each phase there is a gate, or go/no go decision to continue to the next phase or to stop the project. The decision is based on a business case which provides a cost/benefit analysis of the project.

There are quite a few different variations of phase gate: Stage Gate and PACE are two non-proprietary versions. Also, the Rational Unified Process (RUP) has much in common with Phase Gate. Each has its own naming convention, so here I've used some simple, generic names.

Phase Gate starts with a *Concept* phase. Here a few, generally senior people will work with a project manager to do some high-level scoping and planning. Frequently this is done in a few days or a few weeks. The focus is to identify the major requirements, propose a concept for the finished project, and complete the first iteration of the project plan. The plan includes rough schedule and cost estimates which are added to the business case so a decision can be made whether or not to continue with the project.

If things look promising, the project will move into its next phase, *Planning*. Since the planning actually starts in the concept phase, this is really the detailed planning. Work continues on the requirements, but the primary focus is on planning and architecture. At the end it's expected that you will have requirements that are baselined, a solid architecture, and a project plan that people can commit to. Before the OK is given to continue, there may be a lengthy formal review, as major funds will be committed for the development phase.

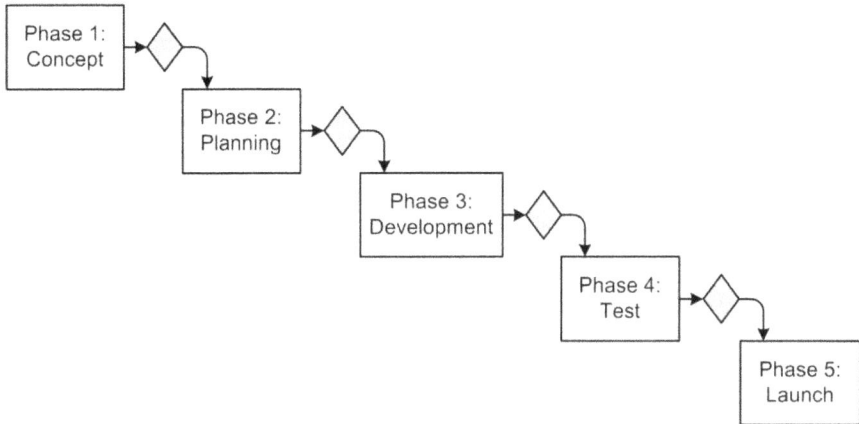

Figure 2.2. The Phase Gate process flow.

If the OK is given, the project moves into the *Development* phase. If you recall all of the deliverables for the printed circuit board, most of them are created during this phase. Also, the development team will also be doing a lot of internal testing before the product is ready to release.

At the end of development, there is a review, and then it moves into the *Test* phase. This is really the formal testing as you will be doing quite a bit of testing during development. Typically this phase might include qualification and acceptance testing, and certification. You're making sure that your product meets all of its specifications so it can move into a product launch, where you have a product that is ready to be marketed and sold.

In most organizations, this marks the end of the project. With the product *Launch*, it is taken out of the hands of development and moved into operations or manufacturing for sale to customers. At least, that is what is supposed to happen. Too often, there is maintenance work required for products that were not quite complete, and, as we will see, this can cause problems when resources are assigned to the next project, but are required to support the shipped product. Their availability is reduced, impacting the current schedule, and they can compromise the quality of their current product.

Agile

Another process that addresses the shortcomings of waterfall is Agile. It was developed to deal with unstable requirements, provide prioritized functionality early, work in self empowered teams, and spend less time on planning and more time responding to the needs of the customers. Like phase gate, there are many flavors of Agile. Scrum is a popular variation. Note that RUP, while being similar to phase gate, is also iterative. Thus phase gate and Agile are not mutually exclusive.

In Agile, a number of features are developed and tested in an iteration (Figure 2.3). The iterations progress sequentially and the final deliverable is incrementally built up. The product of an iteration is fully functional and while it can be released to a customer, generally a release is made after a number of iterations. A large project can also be broken into a number of releases, with each release having a complete Agile development cycle.

Agile projects start with a list of features which are used to create the product vision or project scope and a high level plan. The plan may be no more than a list of the expected iterations with the features planned to be in each iteration. The team structure and the interfaces between people are also laid out and the duration is specified. This process is sometimes referred to as Iteration zero, and it is similar to the concept phase of the phase gate.

With iteration 0 complete, we get to what most people think of when they hear Agile, the iterations to develop the product. Each iteration has a fixed duration, such as 4 weeks, and they proceed sequentially – there is no overlap.

Basically there are three sequential elements within an iteration:

- *Define*: the iteration starts with brief meetings to select the features to be implemented in the iteration, and to produce a detailed plan for the iteration.

- *Develop and Test*: this is the bulk of the work in the iteration, where the selected features are developed and tested. There is a daily meeting to discuss actual and planned progress and issues encountered. After a fixed duration, the completed features are released, providing an incremental improvement to the product.

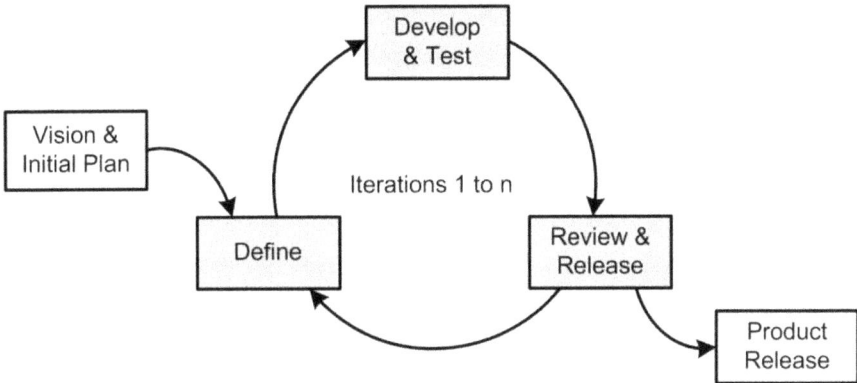

Figure 2.3. The Agile Software Development Process.

- *Review and Release*: the iteration ends with a brief meeting where the results of the iteration are reviewed to compare planned vs. progress. The results are also fed into the *Define* phase of the next iteration to provide constant learning and adaptation, which takes the place of a detailed, up front plan.

As soon as one iteration ends, the next begins. When you've completed all of the iterations, your Product is ready for Release. Here you look back and assess your project to gather information to improve future projects.

There are a number of benefits to Agile that are making it quite popular:

1. Iterative, incremental development
2. Teamwork
3. Performance feedback
4. Direct customer involvement

These benefits are not unique to Agile but, they are inherent in its structure; they are not inherent to waterfall or phase gate.

As we will see, Schedule Centered Planning lays out iterative, incremental development and helps build teamwork. The end of each stage in the strategy also provides the opportunity for performance feedback and for customer involvement with partial deliverables. Thus Schedule Centered Planning could be used to make a waterfall or a phase gate process more Agile-like.

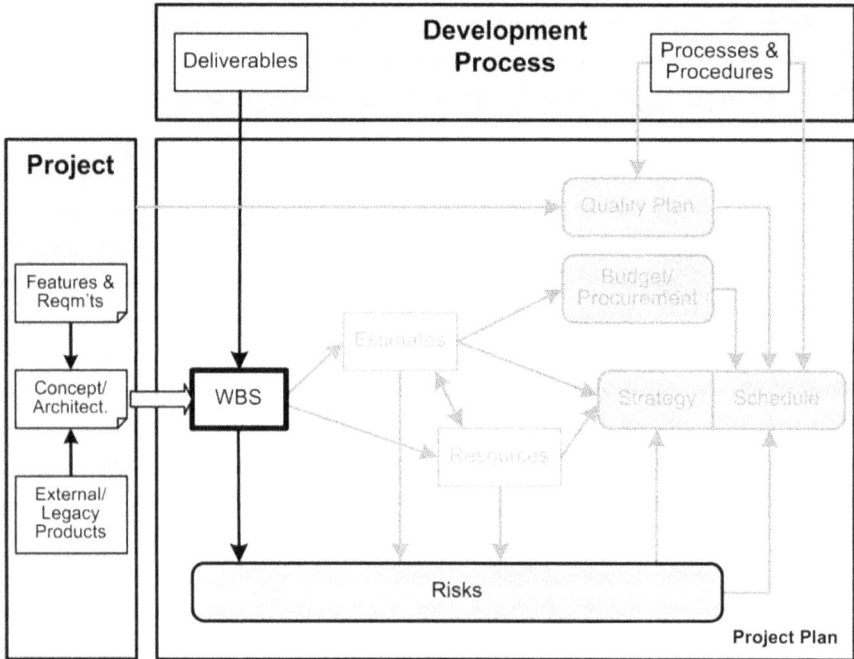

Development Process

Deliverables

Processes & Procedures

Project

Features & Reqm'ts

Concept/ Architect.

External/ Legacy Products

WBS

Quality Plan

Budget/ Procurement

Estimates

Resources

Strategy

Schedule

Risks

Project Plan

3 Break the Work into Pieces: the WBS

What is the WBS?

Planning begins with the Work Breakdown Structure – WBS. This is where we dissect the project to truly understand what has to be done.

The WBS can be defined more formally as: a deliverables-oriented, hierarchical breakdown of project scope, which defines the total work to be performed. From this definition we can define its key attributes:

- The WBS focuses on deliverables – not the tasks to create them;
- It is usually presented as a hierarchy or tree diagram;
- It is a breakdown of scope into smaller pieces; and
- It must define all work.

As the Schedule Centered Planning process flow shows, the WBS is one of the key elements in your project plan. From it: resources are identified to do the work, estimates of work and cost are generated, the strategy is created, and it lays out the detail structure of the schedule. Therefore, criteria to consider while creating your WBS Include:

- The WBS must represent 100% of the work. Anything not in the WBS will not be in the schedule and will cause issues later on when discovered.
- The WBS must be sufficiently detailed so you understand the complexity of the project.
- The components must be broken down far enough for you to make reasonable estimates. When a resource is not sure how long it will take to create a deliverable, then it is frequently useful to break it down further.
- When you start your WBS, i.e. when you start planning, you also start to identify and think about project risks. As we will see, when properly performed, risk analysis and management is concurrent with scheduling.

The WBS must be done right, your entire plan depends on it.

What goes into the WBS?

To better understand the WBS, we can breakdown the work that goes into it:

- All deliverables are either Product specific or Process related. The product is the end product – what is unique about this project. The processes defines how the work is to be performed and what standard deliverables must be produced. The processes are common to all projects.

- The end product of the project is broken down into its Product Breakdown Structure (PBS). First the top level modules are identified; then each module is broken into its components, etc. This is continued until the product is fully understood. That is, can estimates be made and do the assigned resources understand what is to be produced? When either of these cannot be readily answered, then consider further break down of that portion of the PBS.

- The PBS also includes any third party hardware or software required, and components of external projects or products, such as a legacy system, that will be modified. Don't take these for granted. If you do, you might have some unpleasant surprises as the project progresses.

- The Product deliverables also include integration and test, prototypes product specific tests, certification, etc. These are related to or driven by the end product.

- Once the Product portion of the WBS is complete, the Process deliverables are added to it. Foremost among process deliverables is Documentation. All required documents must be identified and then assigned to the appropriate deliverables in the PBS. Here you have to work with key team members to define the required documents and what the scope of each should be. For example, for a simple project there might only be one design document, but for a more complex project each high level module might require its own design document.

- In addition to documentation, your process will generally require Test and Validation of the final product. This can be added along with the product specific testing.

Figure 3.1 shows a tree diagram of what goes into the WBS. While this is not a WBS, it does show what a WBS might look like.

```
                          ┌──────────────┐
                          │     WBS      │
                          └──────┬───────┘
              ┌──────────────────┴──────────────────┐
      ┌───────┴───────┐                      ┌───────┴───────┐
      │    Product    │                      │    Process    │
      └───────┬───────┘                      └───────┬───────┘
      ┌───────┴───────┐                  ┌───────────┴───────────┐
┌─────┴─────┐  ┌──────┴────────┐  ┌──────┴────────┐  ┌───────────┴────┐
│    PBS    │  │Integration/Test│  │ Documentation │  │ Test/Validation │
└───────────┘  └───────────────┘  └───────────────┘  └────────────────┘
```

PBS	Integration/Test	Documentation	Test/Validation
- Module 1	- Integration	- Requirements	- Reviews
- Component 1	Stages	- Design	- Walkthroughs
- Component 2	- Prototypes	- Test Plans	- Inspection
· · ·	- Development	- Test	- Qualification
- Module 2	Systems	Procedures	- Acceptance
· · ·	- Special Tests	· · ·	· · ·
- Legacy	- Certification		
- 3rd Party Items	· · ·		

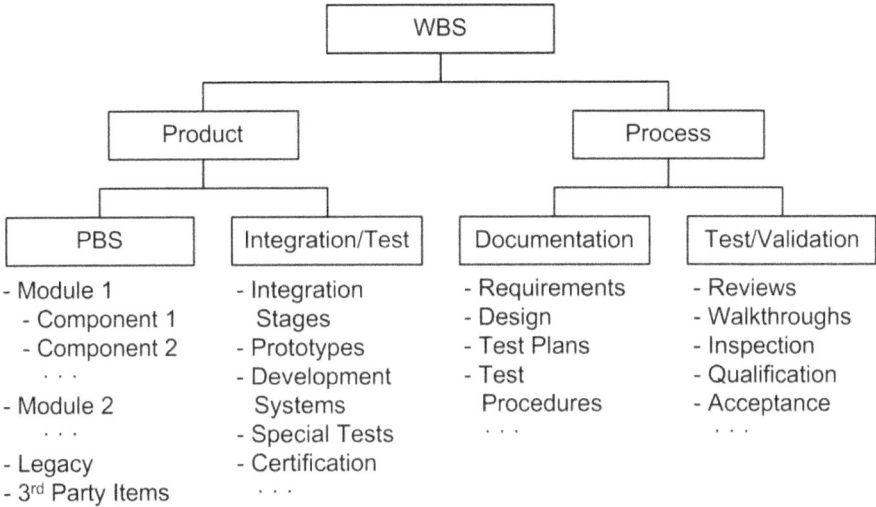

Figure 3.1. What goes into a WBS

Note that by definition, the WBS is deliverables oriented. However, test and certification are included in the WBS, and they are actions, not deliverables. They are included because they are actions that significantly transform a deliverable. The product is not considered the same without the certification as with it.

Create a Process Deliverables Table

Developing a WBS in a multidisciplinary organization can be a daunting task, and it is easy to overlook something. If your projects involve many different groups, you can make your job of creating a WBS easier and eliminate the possibility of overlooking something by creating a table that lists all of the deliverables for each group, such as the one for a printed circuit board in Table 2.1. Then, when your PBS is complete, you can quickly turn it into a WBS.

An Example of a WBS

The best way to understand the WBS is to look at a concrete example. Suppose we have to put together a simple Data Acquisition System (DAS) to monitor a manufacturing process. We can break the DAS into the following major modules:

- Data Acquisition hardware and software to scan input signals and store the raw data in the computer.
- Data Processing to convert the raw data into the correct units (e.g. °F, PSI, etc.) and do calculations with the data to determine process parameters, check alarm limits, etc.
- Display the data in various formats to provide information about the current state of the process.
- Archive data to be able to look at trends and analyze the history of operations.

Each of these is expanded into its components, which is shown in the example PBS in Figure 3.2

This PBS can be expanded into a WBS by adding integration and test and a design document for each major module (Figure 3.3). As you will see, the strategy lays out the integration stages, and each stage should be listed in the WBS. Here three generic stages are listed. In addition, functional and systems tests will be performed, and these will require an integration plan and a test plan.

Note that this WBS is not unique. While for this simple system, I would expect all to be quite similar, or at least have many of the same 3rd level deliverables, it is possible to break it up differently and get a different result.

There are some specific aspects of this WBS that can be noted:

- Under Data Acquisition the DAS Interface is broken into a Basic and a Final DAS Interface. These might have been done for better estimates or in anticipation of the strategy where a simple, basic DAS is created first for an early deliverable, and to be used for the development and test of the other deliverables.

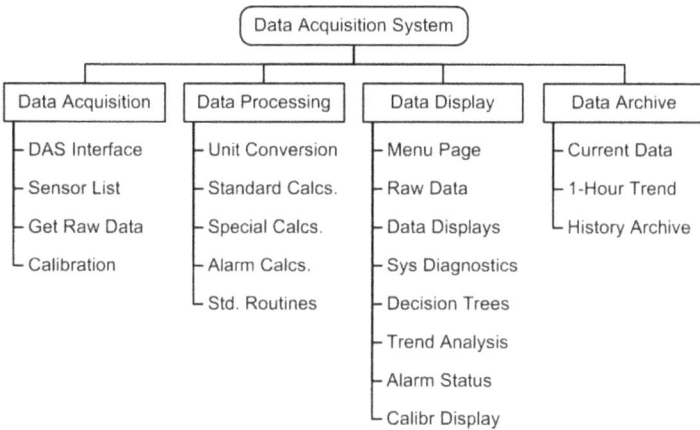

Figure 3.2 A PBS for a Data Acquisition System

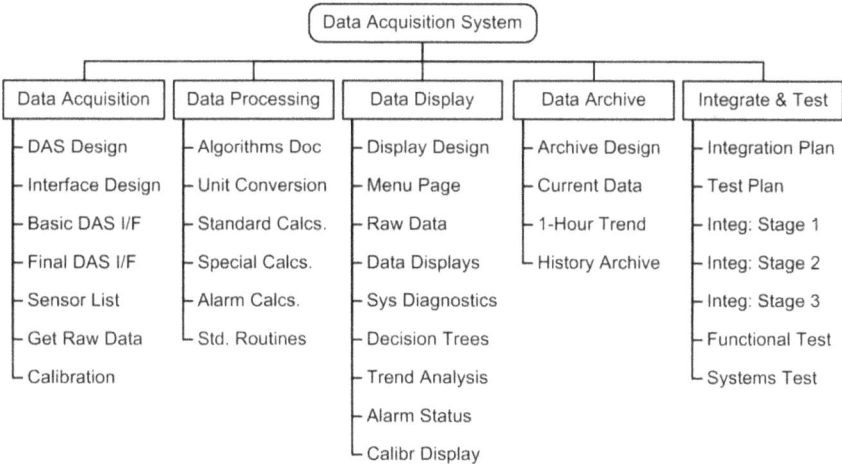

Figure 3.3 Expanding the DAS PBS into a WBS

- Similarly, in Data Processing there are Standard Calculations and Special Calculations. The two sets of calculations might be for better estimating, to spread the work in different stages of the strategy, or because the Special Calculations require a specific resource to code the complex algorithms.

- Under Integrate and Test are three generic integration stages. The actual stages will be identified in Chapter 6, when we identify the integration strategy for the DAS.

17

Timing and the WBS

The WBS is not a timing diagram – it is not meant to depict timing. However, there is a tendency to infer timing when reading from left to right and from top to bottom. Therefore, the design documents (e.g. DAS Design) are listed first under each of the high level deliverables because these are the first things done for each deliverable. It's good to put deliverables that are done first over to the left, or at the top of a list; those done last are at right or the bottom. Doing this will make your work easier when you move the WBS into your schedule, and the resulting Gantt chart will look better with a general flow from upper left to lower right.

Assigning Owners to Deliverables

The WBS is a good place to show ownership. As resources are assigned to your project, you should assign an owner to each major deliverable. The owner will be responsible for the deliverable, doing most, and frequently all of the work, and will provide a single point of contact for questions and answers. Here I would assign an owner to Data Acquisition, Data Processing, etc. For a larger project you may have to go down a level to assign owners. Here for example, Special Calculations might require a different owner than Data Processing.

Start Identifying Risk While Developing the WBS

As pointed out in the introduction, it's important to start identifying risks while creating the WBS. First we have to define risk:

$$Risk = Uncertainty$$

This is as basic as you can get, but uncertainty is the key word in any definition of risk. And what this tells us is that:

$$Uncertainty = Risk$$

So, rather than ask specifically about risk, you should be looking for areas of uncertainty. As you're creating your WBS, you should be getting information from those resources already assigned to the project. For each deliverable ask them simple questions like:

- What's unique about this?
- What do you see is a challenge?
- What could cause this deliverable to be late?

Sometimes you don't even have to ask them the questions. Uncertainty will be clear from their descriptions. When they indicate a problem area, follow up on it. This is really an ongoing conversation you have with your team members during planning. Asking them questions forces them to think about potential risks, something they may not do on their own.

Don't expect answers right away. It's more important for them to think about the questions for a while. If something comes to mind, they will come back to you. That way you will get more useful information.

The worst thing to do is to prompt for answers, especially the answers you really want to hear. Once an answer is given, it can shut down the continued thinking that might produce something you really need to know.

Other WBS risks to consider

For both software and hardware in your WBS, consider the major interfaces. They may be internal to the project or they may be to an external system. These have the potential for risk. Assumptions have to be made about how things should behave, but frequently, reality shows that these assumptions were wrong.

Third-party software is another area where you can run into surprises because of wrong assumptions. Make sure you know what's involved in bringing up and integrating third party software – what are the potential problems? They could be related to size, performance or functionality. The sooner you identify these problems, the easier they are to deal with.

And procured deliverables in general are a potential risk. We'll discuss these in more detail when we discuss Procurement.

Don't get bogged down in details

Another pitfall when identifying risk is getting bogged down in detail. Any project has lots of little uncertainties, and these tend to get resolved during the course of execution. What you want to focus on during early planning are the major uncertainties that can seriously challenge your project. I call these the show stopper risks. As we will see, these drive your effort estimates and your strategy.

Do not just ignore the lesser risks. Note them in the risk log so you can return to them later in the planning.

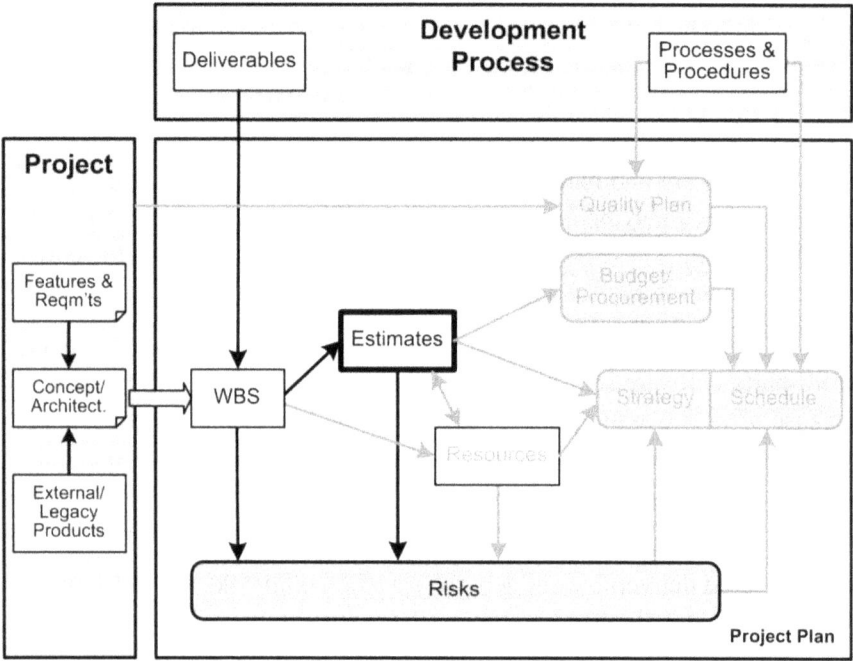

4 What Will it Take: Estimating

Estimating is one of the more challenging aspects of planning. Estimates may be generated by comparing the current project with past projects, by breaking the project down to low level activities or by applying an appropriate model. As you plan you should use a few different approaches, make multiple estimates, refine them as you gather more information and check them for consistency.

During planning, you will typically make the following estimates:

- *Top-down*: An early, rough estimate based on scope and a concept, which uses similarity to past projects or a model that has been verified by past projects.

- *Bottom-up*: Based on requirements and an early architecture, estimates are made for the lowest elements in the PBS or WBS and rolled up.

- *Schedule*: A more detailed bottom-up estimate – the WBS deliverables are expanded to include the tasks needed to create them.

Top-down Estimates

Top-down estimates are the initial, rough sizing estimates you make for your project. Not a lot is known – typically just the key requirements and a concept or idea of how they might be implemented. With this you identify the major deliverables and other important aspects of the project. For our data acquisition software you might start with the top level deliverables:

- Data Acquisition
- Data Processing
- Data Display
- Data Archive
- Integration and Test

Then experienced people estimate how much work will be required for each based on similarity to past projects. Although rough, these estimates can be very important:

- To assess if the project is worth doing

- To understand the size and complexity of the project
- To estimate how many resources you need

To assure they are reasonable, don't just ask for an estimate of total work. Many people will give you the first number that pops into their head which may or may not be meaningful. Rather, ask questions about size and complexity first, to get them to start thinking. Typical questions might be:

- What were some similar past projects?
- How complex were those projects?
- What were the biggest challenges?
- Will the challenges be similar or different on this project?
- Are specific resources required to do any of the work?

As you ask these questions, don't be in a hurry for answers. Be quiet and give people time to think. In fact, suggest that they take the time to think about it and get back to you at a later time. You will get a lot more information, and the estimates will be more meaningful.

Bottom-up Estimates

When you've completed your WBS, you know a lot more about your project. The top level deliverables are broken down into smaller pieces. Now you can estimate the work for the lowest level deliverables and roll the totals up to create a bottom-up estimate. As with the top-down estimates, discuss size and complexity first by asking questions similar to the ones for the top-down estimates.

Schedule Estimates

Your schedule starts with your WBS and you add the tasks needed to create each deliverable. You will also add activities for dealing with:

- risk
- quality – e.g. design reviews
- procurement – e.g. preparation tasks and lead times
- support – e.g. setting up special hardware, test systems or prototypes.

You will also generate estimates for the individual tasks, sequence the tasks, and level the resources. This gives you a bottom-up estimate with much finer granularity with a schedule you can commit to.

Some Simple Rules to Assure Good Estimates

- As you're creating your WBS you should assign resources to each deliverable. Each resource should estimate the work they will do. People will not commit to an estimate they did not make.

- When you are given an estimate, make sure that you understand what it means. If somebody says a deliverable will take six weeks, what will you have at the end of that six weeks? They might not include all of the work. If I feel the number is low I'll ask: "What does this six weeks include?" I might find that a resource assumes he can take a shortcut – e.g. do a design on a whiteboard rather than produce a document that can be reviewed and released. Knowing this, we work together to update the estimate.

- Never prompt somebody for a desired answer. Don't say things like: "Do you think you can do this in three weeks?" You might hear what you want to hear, but it's your number, the individual will not feel like she is making a commitment.

- Beware of people giving you a number that they think you want to hear. They assume they are doing you a favor but they're not. The schedule might look good but you will run into problems when you get in to the execution where you have fewer options to resolve the problems. It's always best to identify and deal with issues early.

- When you see that a person is struggling to come up with an estimate, accept that and see what you can do. You might try to break the deliverable into smaller pieces, or identify somebody else who might have a better understanding and can help them. Again, resolve the uncertainty as soon as possible.

- Consider what groups or functional areas are not addressed in early estimates. For example, engineers can have a tendency to overlook quality assurance (QA). However, QA work is generally proportionate to engineering work. In one organization, by looking at time card data, we found that the ratio of development engineers to QA engineers to be 1:1 for small projects and 2:1 for large projects. This is useful for early QA estimates.

Work vs. Duration When Estimating

Estimates represent work while your schedule is all about duration. A two week task is 80 hours of work – that is, two weeks is the duration if you have one person working 8 hours per day. However, the resource might not be able to work 8 hours per day on your project. She might have to support other projects, or perform routine maintenance. So you have to also know the availability of the resource doing the task. If she is only available 80%, then this task will actually have 12.5 days duration. Similarly, if the same resource has a total of 4 months of work with 80% availability, it will take her 5 months to complete. This will add a month to your schedule – a significant impact on your end date.

Don't forget holidays, vacation, and other nonworking time. They also push out your schedule. If a resource has 10 holidays and 4 weeks of vacation per year, this can add 3 or more weeks to a 6 month project.

Estimating Models

Estimating models take parameters describing a particular project and convert these into a rough estimate of total effort or duration. An applicable model can improve estimates when doing top-down or bottom-up estimating, especially when based on historical data. Parameters you might have to gather include:

- Inputs and Outputs
- Database tables
- Queries
- Files
- Web pages
- Etc.

Typically you provide a count of small, medium and large elements, and identify other characteristics that correct for complexity. Gathering this type of information has the added advantage of looking at size and complexity rather than effort.

There are many models, each of which applies to a specific type of project, and all are too detailed to be discussed here. I highly recommend the book by Steve McConnell (see References at the end of this chapter) which discusses a fair number of models.

Planning Poker

I have stressed the importance of thinking about size and complexity before making estimates. Planning poker is used by Agile teams to estimate the relative size of features in the product backlog. A similar process can be used when creating bottom-up estimates from the PBS.

When used with a PBS, it forces quantifying size and complexity first, and provides an excellent opportunity to bring the entire team together to develop an intimate understanding about the entire project. The project manager should also listen during the discussions for potential risks that might be uncovered. As risk analysis is not the intended purpose, these can be addressed following the completion of the planning poker session.

Each person is given a deck of cards, where each card has a number representing relative size. A typical scheme uses numbers from the Fibonacci sequence: 1, 2, 3, 5, 8, 13 and 21. Then the lowest level deliverables in the PBS or WBS are ranked by relative size and complexity by assigning an appropriate number to each.

A good time to do this is when you have completed the PBS. All assigned team members should be present along with a few experienced non-team members who understand the technical areas being covered. The deliverables are listed, and there may be brief discussion or questions. Since the sizing is relative, it is useful to identify the smallest deliverables first, agree which is the smallest, and assign a value of 1 or 2. All others will be evaluated relative to this deliverable. Alternatively, the deliverables can be sorted and those in the middle assigned a value of 5 or 8. Then, moving out from the middle the smaller and then the larger deliverables are assigned a number based on size and complexity.

When considering a deliverable, the owner of that deliverable provides a brief description and, if possible, similarities to prior projects. Others present are then free to ask questions. When all questions have been answered, each person is asked to select one card representing the relative size/complexity of the deliverable. Relative is based on those deliverables which already have an assigned number. When all have decided, the cards are displayed. Most of the time there will be a range of numbers, and those who suggest the highest and the lowest discuss what they know and what they assume that drives their assessment. That is, why is the high number and the low number warranted. These are discussed until consensus is reached, which might require a second round of the planning poker.

For the DAS, the WBS has 32 deliverables Sorting this can be tedious. However, each of the major deliverables has eight or fewer deliverables which are related. These can be quickly sorted and then merged together. It's not necessary to be precise, as positions might change when values are assigned to all elements.

With deliverables sized and sorted, estimates can be made of the total amount of work.

Historical Data

Early estimates generally rely on past experience. Since the memory of that experience might be imperfect or those with the experience have left the organization, maintaining historical data is the best way to preserve important information from past projects. Then, it is always available and does not change over time.

As a minimum, an historical database must record the original estimates and the actual work or duration for each project. Other relevant project characteristics, such as type, size, complexity or relevant modeling parameters allow you to be more specific when choosing past projects for comparison. This data can directly help you with your estimates, or the ratio of actual work to estimated work for past projects can improve an independent estimate. For example, if the average ratio of actual to estimated work for recent projects is 1.25, then you should add 25% to your current estimate.

When you're starting a new project, you use historical data to choose the projects most relevant to your project and use the data to estimate effort and duration. Just don't forget to make adjustments for the resources assigned to the current project relative to the resources that were assigned to the previous projects. Then, when a new project is started, the information associated with its estimates is added to the database; upon completion, the actual data is added.

If you must create a database from scratch, when choosing how much data to save, more might be good, but more may not be better. Like so many things, there is a quantum leap when you go from nothing to something simple. Adding complexity is then just an incremental improvement. When you characterize things like size and complexity, keep it simple: use three levels such as low, medium or high.

Example of a simple database

Here is a really simple database put together by a couple of project managers. We went through old projects where we had both a baseline and a final schedule, and extracted the initial and final engineering work estimates. With a dozen projects, the results were quite surprising, as shown in the table below.

	Effort (person-months)		
	Initial	Final	Ratio
Project 1	15.3	17.2	1.1
Project 2	10.4	21.4	2.1
Project 3	8.3	21.9	2.6
Project 4	10.7	21.9	2.0
Project 5	31.2	25.4	0.8
Project 6	17.0	30.4	1.8
Project 7	21.0	32.4	1.5
Project 8	19.3	35.7	1.8
Project 9	31.4	46.8	1.5
Project 10	35.2	68.2	1.9
Project 11	78.8	79.9	1.0
Project 12	73.5	111.8	1.5
		Average:	1.7

Table 4.1. Data from a simple historical database.

The first thing to note is that out of 12 projects, only one (Project 5) required less effort than originally planned. And not a lot less! Two more were close to the initial estimate, but the remaining projects were quite a bit higher. Unfortunately, this is typical in new product development.

On average, the ratio of the final effort to the initial estimate was 1.7, with a couple running at more than twice the original estimate. None of us would have guessed that, in general, estimates were off by 70%! A brainstorming session revealed three causes for the overruns:

- Baselining too soon: 10-20%
- Optimistic estimates:20-30%
- Scope creep: 20-40%, sometimes more

These three issues were listed previously when discussing uncertainty in estimates. By better understanding these issues, subsequent estimates were improved, frequently by adding contingency to the early estimates.

A review of the data, showed it is possible to partition it into three sizes with an average work estimate for each size:

#	Size	Average Work
1-5:	Small	22 person-months
6-9:	Medium	36 person-months
10-12:	Large	80 person-months

Then, an early characterization of a project as small, medium or large provides a pretty good estimate of the work required. The error will be less than 25% most of the time, which is pretty good for such an early estimate. It's also a lot better than the 70% average error in the actual data! This is very useful when you have to choose from a number of potential projects. You can quickly generate a reasonable estimate for each.

Although not shown in the table, each project was also characterized by a major and minor type, to make it easier to choose those most similar to a new project. We did not have any convenient metrics for size or complexity, but these tend to be related to the major and minor types, so including them would not have made a significant improvement.

The bottom line: even a limited database can be extremely useful. Combining this with data like the average ratio of QA engineers to development engineers discussed earlier, can significantly improve early estimates. And it's not a lot of work!.

Uncertainty in Estimates

As you go from the rough top-down estimates to the detailed schedule estimates, the uncertainty decreases. Recalling that uncertainty is risk, the best way to reduce your schedule risks is to improve your estimates.

The environment where you work will also have a major impact on your estimates. Working in new product development with mechanical, electrical and software engineers, I have found that estimates tend to be on the low side. Looking back over many completed projects I've identified three major causes of under-estimating.

1. Baselining the schedule before the work is fully understood. This may be unavoidable on large, complex projects since management needs a delivery estimate in a reasonable amount of time.

2. Optimistic estimates. Estimates tend to be overly ambitious or success oriented, not foreseeing the difficulties that will arise.

3. Scope creep. Frequently unavoidable since it adds needed functionality to the finished product.

You might have similar challenges to deal with, or you may work with resources who tend to overestimate – that is, they add some protective padding. You have to know your environment.

Range Estimates

Early on, I like to gather range estimates rather than single numbers. After discussing size and complexity, when I ask for an estimate, I take that to be a nominal value. I follow that estimate up with a question such as: "But what is the worst case?" Then, when I am pushed to make an early prediction, I base it on the range estimates, and, in my environments, I present the worst-case first. So, if the range of estimates is 6 to 8 months, I might say: "It will take 8 months, but we are trying to pull it in to 7 months" or "we're trying to pull it in to 6 months", whichever I'm most comfortable with.

In some environments basing predictions on the worst case can be problematic, such as when bidding a contract. Here, to provide reasonable estimates, you have to do the due diligence to get a reasonable most likely estimate, and not just go with the nominal estimates. Again, you should not have to do this for too many deliverables.

Three Point Estimates

When I have a reasonably mature WBS and start generating bottom-up estimates, I'll expand the range estimate to a 3-point estimate by asking for a best case or optimistic estimate along with the worst case. While the numbers are important, the assumptions behind those estimates are just as important. Along with the optimistic estimate I might ask: "What would it take to pull it in to that value?" Most of the time, I'll learn that the optimistic estimate is just a smaller number and if they're lucky, they might be able to achieve it. But occasionally I'm told that if they had an early version of a document, or preliminary code that somebody else is working on, it will save them a week or two. This is very useful information because, as project manager, I might be able to make those things happen.

Similarly, when I get the worst case estimate, I'll ask: "What could cause that to happen?" Knowing what can cause a slip, I might be able to prevent it from happening, or at least minimize the impact.

For most of the deliverables, the initial estimate is roughly in the middle between the optimistic and the worst case, and does not differ greatly from them (Figure 4.1a). Also, it's rare, for the initial estimate to be closer to the worst case than to the optimistic. So what you are looking for are those few cases, and hopefully it's only a few, where there is a large gap between the initial estimate and the worst case (Figure 4.1b). These can have a major impact on your schedule. And you probably know which deliverables they are since you started to identify risks when creating the WBS.

Once you have a problematic worst case, rather than discussing assumptions you need to discuss scenarios – identify the problems and walk through how they may impact the development. On a few occasions, when discussing scenarios with team members, the worst case starts to push further and further out. This can happen when the nominal estimates are based on unreal optimism. There is an unstated assumption that nothing will go wrong as team members visualize how everything will go just right. By spending time discussing worst case scenarios, it changes their focus. Then, a potential disaster can be identified early, you can address it in your plan and you have more flexibility in dealing with it. But be patient, it may take a few days of hard thinking to consider all possibilities. Give the resources the time that they need.

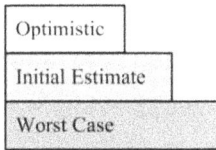

Figure 4.1a. A typical 3-point distribution

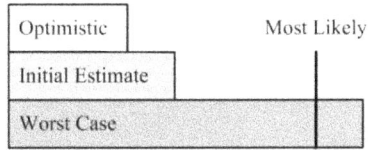

Figure 4.1b. A problematic 3-point distribution

After going through the worst case scenarios identify activities, such as an early prototype, that can mitigate the impact. Add the necessary work to the deliverable and reevaluate the worst case scenarios, assess the likelihood of any one of them happening, and estimate the most likely value which is somewhere between your updated estimate and the worst case.

Reference

I highly recommend the book: *Software Estimating: Demystifying the Black Art* by Steve McConnell. This book contains a wealth of information which is useful even if you don't manage software.

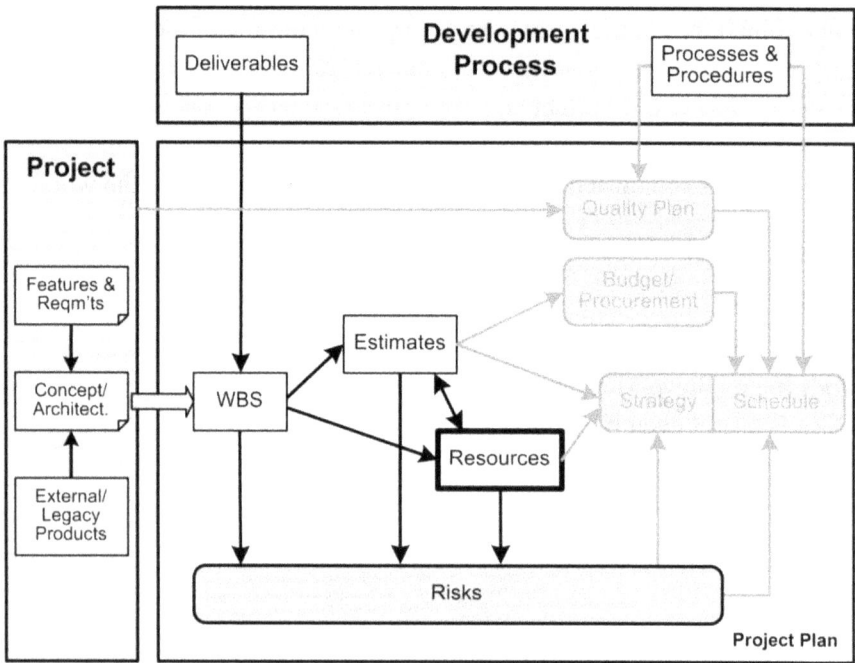

Development Process

Deliverables

Processes & Procedures

Project

Features & Reqm'ts

Concept/ Architect.

External/ Legacy Products

WBS

Estimates

Quality Plan

Budget/ Procurement

Resources

Strategy

Schedule

Risks

Project Plan

5 Who Will Do It: Resources

Resources are a key element of your project – they do the work, they bring success. Some resources may be assigned to your project early, while others have to be acquired based on the needs you've identified during early planning.

The Right Team

You can identify most of your resource needs when you start defining the deliverables in your WBS. As you're identifying the top level deliverables ask yourself a number of key questions:

What skills are required to do this?

Are there a number of people who can do the work or will I need a specific resource? For example, within a software group you might need somebody who knows networking interface protocols, and there are only two people in your organization who do this. Then you don't have a lot of leeway.

What skill level is required? Does it have to be a senior person or can somebody with limited experience do the job? Be realistic! It might be nice to have mostly senior resources on your project, but they are usually in high demand. Identify those areas where you absolutely have to have somebody with lots of experience. As you may have to fight for that resource, you want to save your energy for where it really counts.

What work can readily be assigned to a junior level resource? It's generally easier to get junior people than senior people. So this is a good way to build up your team, especially if you feel that you are under resourced.

Assign Owners

As team members are assigned to your project, you should assign owners to the deliverables in the WBS. Each high level deliverable should have an owner – a single person you can go to for questions about that deliverable. While frequently assigned to the top level elements, for a larger deliverable or one that is a collection of deliverables, such as test and integrate, here you can assign owners at the next level down.

Generally the owner will do the work, but other resources may be required for specific tasks or to help with the work. For the Data Acquisition System, I would initially assign a separate owner to each of the high level deliverables: Data Acquisition, Data Processing, Data Display and Data Archive. Each owner is responsible for the breakdown and all estimates for the assigned deliverable.

Once you have owners assigned, work with them to expand the high level deliverable and create the bottom-up estimates. This gives you a better estimate of the total work. Also, compare the workload of all of the resources to see if one or more resources have too much work. If you do have a major imbalance, first try to add more resources to the project. Here is good place to identify where junior resources can pick up the load. Then see if it's possible to share the work. It may not seem possible when the work is highly specialized, but if you work with the individuals involved, they can get quite creative. Resource leveling is part of scheduling, but if you can get the resources reasonably leveled here, then when you get to the schedule your job will be a lot easier. (We'll do this for the DAS when we discuss the schedule.)

Integrate and test is a collection of deliverables. As project manager, I frequently generate the integration plan with input from the team members, so I recommend that the PM own it. The Test Plan, Functional Test and Systems Test would be owned by a QA resource. Each integration stage would be assigned to one of the primary deliverable owners based on the nature of the integration. Here availability is also a consideration since I would not assign responsibility to somebody who is overloaded.

Assigning ownership at a high level in the WBS makes it easier to plan, especially to resource and level the schedule, and it creates a solid project team, one where every person understands his or her responsibilities.

Resource Availability

Skills and experience are important to the success of a project. But, just as important is resource availability.

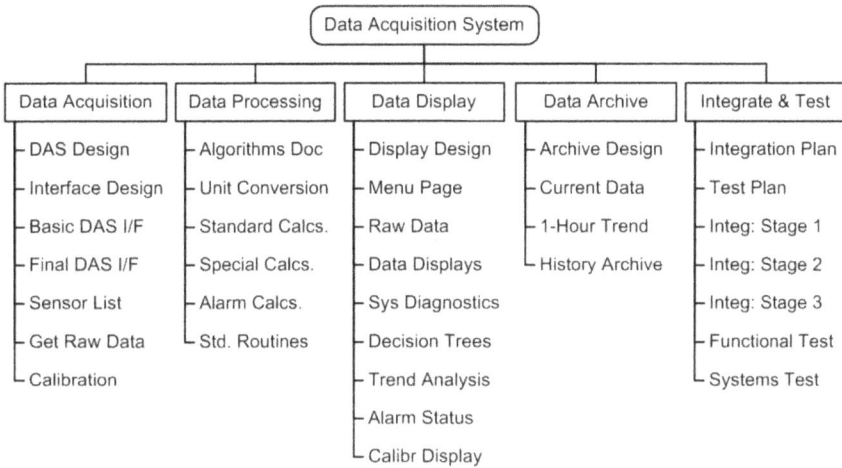

Figure 5.1 The DAS WBS.

Can the resources start when you need them, that is, when your schedule says they must start? When resources start late, this pushes out their work and impacts how they interface with others.

Will they be able to work on your project 100%? When resources multitask, not only do you have to plan for reduced effort, but regularly switching context between two or more projects lowers efficiency. This increases the likelihood of making a mistake. Then, time wasted fixing those mistakes further lowers efficiency. Since multitasking is a reality project managers have to deal with, the best way to deal with it is to have realistic estimates for productivity in your schedule. This way you do not stretch overloaded resources. When you pressure resources to make up for the lost time, that starts the downward spiral of errors that will require more time in the long run, and, it will likely result in a poor quality product being released. (See Do It Right at the end of the Quality Chapter.)

You may have to consider replacing a late or partially available resource. Then you have to look at the skills, experience and availability of the alternates. If those available are less experienced, the work will take longer and the durations will increase. Thus there is the possibility that the end date might not be pulled in and you might be adding risk. So before you swap out a resource, do some what-ifs with your schedule. Of course, if you do decide to swap resources, the new resource will have to update all of the estimates.

Roles and Responsibilities

Project team members must fully understand their roles and responsibilities. Just as the WBS must represent 100% of the work, resource assignments must also cover 100% of the assigned work. To do this, the resources must understand the totality of their work. A useful analogy is that a project is a lot like a jigsaw puzzle where you have to make the individual pieces and then put them together. Many of the problems you encounter are from incorrectly fabricated pieces – they don't fit together – and some might even seem to come from a different puzzle. This is shown in Figure 5.2 on the opposite page.

The interfaces can be a big problem. Occasionally a resource might omit something, assuming it is being done by the other resource. Or there may be mismatched interfaces, like somebody trying to put a square peg into a round hole. These do not happen often, but they can really mess up a schedule, so interface responsibilities must be well understood.

Sometimes you have a resource who doesn't want to do all of the work, feeling that he shouldn't have to do it. For example, a senior resource might balk at doing the more mundane tasks, such as extensive testing of their work. They might say that all testing should be done by QA. Others will try to avoid doing documentation, or will try to get by with incomplete documents. You will have to either push them or get another resource who can help them do the work. It all depends on what that work is.

While it is hard to eliminate these issues, you can minimize them by making sure all of the resources understand where they fit in. It's essential that all interfaces be properly partitioned, well designed and understood by all involved. For complex interfaces, this definitely means creating appropriate documentation, and the key word here is appropriate.

Assigning owners to the elements in the WBS is really only part of laying out responsibilities. As we'll shortly see, the next big step is assigning resources within the strategy. Recall that the WBS breaks down the project and the Strategy puts it all together. So these two are complementary and together show how all of the resources fit into the big picture.

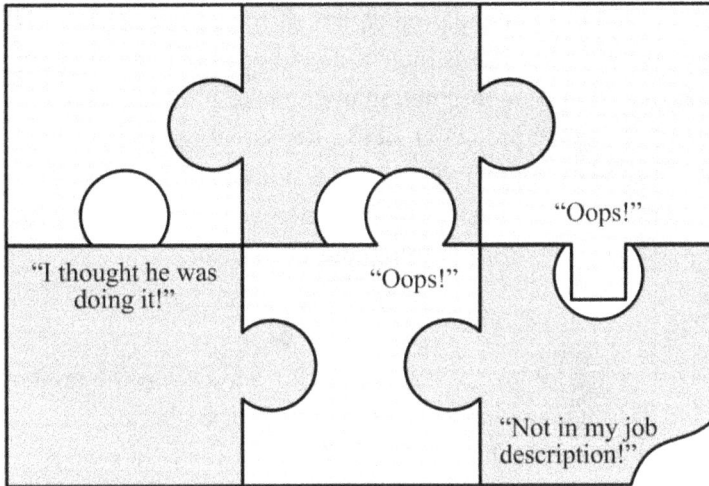

Figure 5.2. The pieces of your project puzzle might not fit together and might be missing functionality.

Multiple Locations

Having resources in multiple locations is another challenge to deal with. First of all, when planning, make sure the work is properly partitioned. In the puzzle analogy, when there is a complex interface shared between two developers, try to make them co-located. If this is not possible, then add time to develop and review a detailed interface design document.

It is also important to get the teams together. Periodic, face-to-face meeting are valuable, but sometimes you don't have the travel budget to make them happen. Video conferencing is the next best thing; it allows team members to associate names with real people. This creates a more personal working relationship. However, once people have met, conference calls can be quite useful for routine status meetings. In fact, they can be better than video conferencing. With video, you just watch the people on the screen fidgeting in their chairs; and they are doing the same to you.

For sharing information, there are a number of software packages for online meetings, such as WebEx and Go to Meeting.

When one location is the prime location, that is they take the lead, it's easy for them to assume that their counterparts at the other locations are fully knowledgeable about the project. However, when those in the other locations do not fully understand the project, it is difficult for them to fully contribute. This may cause friction as their work is not what those in the prime location expect. Therefore, it's important to make sure that there is equal understanding about the project at all locations. Setting up early, informal discussions and question and answer sessions are the best way to deal with this. Not only do they share vital information, but they also help to build a more personal relationship throughout the project.

Team Building

Team building starts when all involved help develop and review the project plan. It is essential to bring people into the planning process because they have the information you need, and it is the best way to assure buy-in of the completed plan. They help to create the WBS and then provide the associated work estimates. The team will have a lot to say about the Strategy, and when you expand it all into a schedule, the resources doing the work will also have to tell you what specific tasks are required. Team members also provide most of your risk information.

Junior members on the team might struggle with the planning. If there is uncertainty or hesitation, you are likely to see it when they are giving estimates or when helping to create the detailed schedule. You should work with senior members or with their management to bring them along, so they understand all of the tasks. Try not to dictate to them. When things get tight, they might say that this was your schedule, not theirs, and not feel any obligation to meet the Milestones.

In addition to planning, it's also beneficial when team members understand the business value of the project. When they can see that the final product is useful, that it can make a difference to the customers and to the organization, these are great motivators.

Finally, make sure that the project team fully accepts the final baselined plan, especially the schedule and the milestones. They are the ones who are responsible for meeting those milestones, so there needs to be acceptance. But even more, there needs to be commitment. The milestones should be owned by the project team.

Project baselining is usually done at a kickoff meeting. However, since the project team has already started working together, and has been responsible for creating the plan, this is more of a team energizing exercise. So it's more important to assure that management and customers are present. They can see the magnitude of the project and appreciate the work done so far. They should discuss the value of and need for the project, review the schedule and resource requirements, and commit to provide what is needed. Their support is essential for project success.

Resource Risks

We've already discussed the sources for major resource issues: having the right team, resource availability, roles and responsibilities, and dealing with multiple locations. They all present the potential for risks. As you are assigning resources to deliverables consider:

- What are your concerns?
- What are you unsure of?
- Do you have a resource on a critical function without sufficient experience?
- Etc.

Note that when you have to use a less experienced resource, there is not only the question of how long the work will take, but also the question of whether the work can be completed. If a resource does not have the necessary skills, he can spend a lot of time to accomplish very little. Eventually, another resource will have to help or complete the work. This will result in a significant delay to the project. So this is something you have to think about carefully when assigning a resource that does not have the proper skills or skill level. What is their potential for growth?

Generally, the risks identified will be associated with the deliverable to which the resource has been assigned. As we'll see, when you've finalized your assignments, it's good to associate the resource risks with those deliverables.

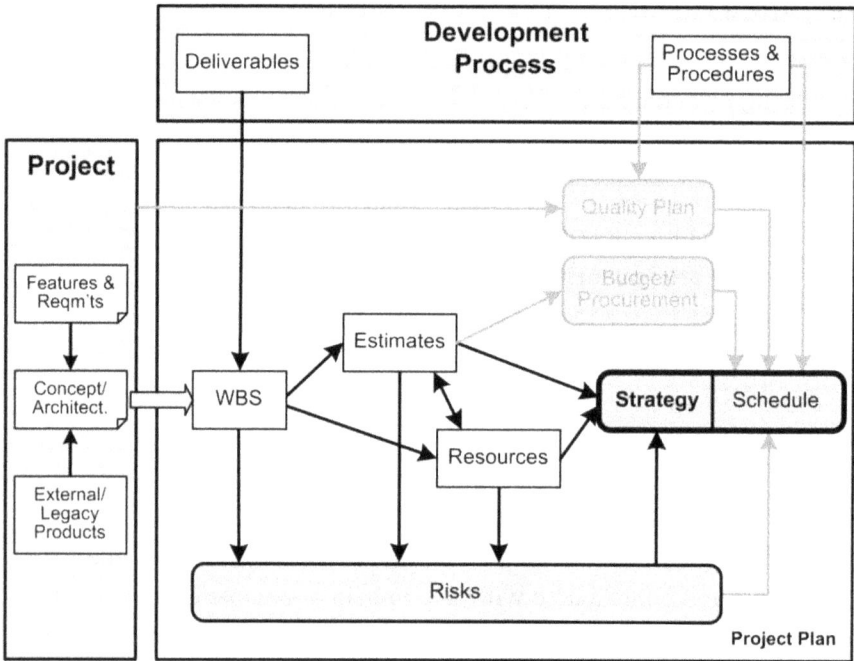

Development Process

Deliverables | Processes & Procedures

Project

Features & Reqm'ts

Concept/ Architect.

External/ Legacy Products

WBS

Estimates

Resources

Quality Plan

Budget/ Procurement

Strategy | Schedule

Risks

Project Plan

6 The Big Picture: Your Strategy

Big picture, strategic thinking is essential for project success. Without it you risk getting bogged down in the details, missing early problem indicators and not making the most effective project decisions. It's easy to go from one crisis to the next, becoming a firefighter rather than a project manager. You want to be in control of your project, not allow it to be in control of you.

Your strategy provides the big picture: it's your game plan, a high level view of your schedule. It is critical to your overall planning because you have to step back and look at the total project. The other aspects of planning involve gathering and processing the details.

In its simplest form, the strategy might be no more than a number of well-defined internal milestones that break up the project timeline. Each milestone must be meaningful and measurable. That is, each must represent the creation of something useful, and it must be easy to establish that everything that was planned to be done has been done.

If you're building a house your first milestone might be that the foundation is complete; the second that the frame is complete. Each of these is both meaningful and measurable. They are essential for building the house, and you can check if either is complete. Also, when the foundation is complete you can start the framing, and when the framing is complete you can start other tasks, such as wiring.

Generally the strategy is more complex. Recall, when you develop your PBS you break down the end product into a number of pieces. Now you consider how best to develop and integrate those pieces together. That is, you consider how to incrementally build-up your end product. This incremental approach has much in common with Agile. However, the work to produce each increment need not fit into a fixed time box and increments can be longer than one month. Also, on a major project it might take three or more months to do the upfront work, referred to as iteration 0.

Process deliverables such as documents are not addressed in your strategy. These are added later, when you create your schedule.

A Strategy for the Data Acquisition System

To better understand what a strategy is, let's look at one for the Data Acquisition System. Generally, we want to start off with something simple. Since the computer will have to interface to hardware, it's good to get a basic interface working as soon as possible. With this simple end-to-end system you have the computer talking to the hardware and something the developers can build on.

With this you might decide to build the system through a series of stages:

1. *Basic Data Acquisition:* Use the DAS to acquire a few pre-chosen data channels and display that data.

2. *Full Data Acquisition:* Set up DAS to scan data at variable timing according to a sensor list, convert the data into meaningful units (e.g. °F, PSI etc.), with basic displays of the converted data.

3. *Special Data Calculations:* Complete all data processing and view with special displays.

4. *Alarm and Trend Analysis:* Store trend and archive data and view with trend and archive displays.

5. *Calibration:* Perform on-line calibration of sensors and store the data in the sensor list.

In Figure 6.1 (opposite) each stage has a descriptive name, the start date, the duration and a number of deliverables from the WBS feeding into it. Looking at stage 1, what this says is that:

- Basic DAS Interface, Get Raw Data and Raw Data Display pieces are first developed and then integrated together

- Integration is planned to start on March 3rd

- The duration for test and integration is expected to be 5 days

Also, it was decided that since sensor calibration is not critical to the other development, it can go as the last stage. Generally reasonable conversion coefficients are known for each sensor type, and with these all of the other functionality will work and can be fully tested. As the diagram shows, it is done in parallel with the Alarm and Trend Analysis. While this is reasonable, as you learn more, you might move it around, making it in series, or in parallel with stage 3, or even combine it with another stage.

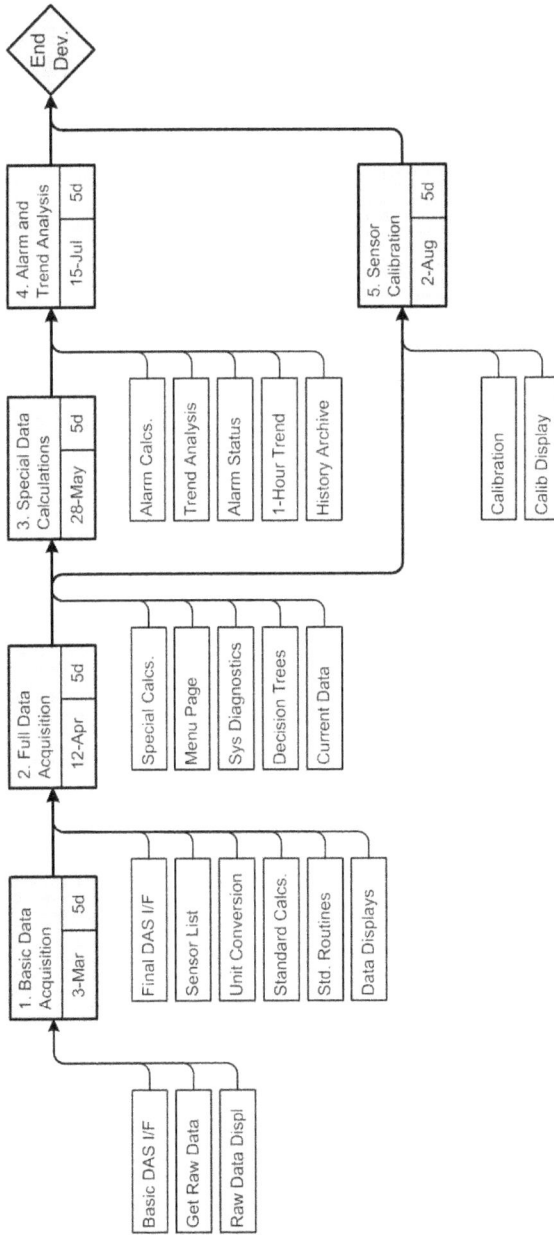

Figure 6.1. A potential strategy for DAS development.

There are advantages to incremental development not shown on the diagram. At the end of the second stage you have the basic data acquisition functionality and this is a good time to start overnight and weekend testing. This burn-in will identify many problems that simple testing will miss. Also, by the end of the third stage, Special Data Calculations, you have the most commonly used features to monitor the process. If users are available, they can start testing here. Continuous testing starting at an early stage will assure that you have a solid, reliable system for delivery. You're building one of the main advantages of Agile into your non-Agile development.

Laying Out Your Strategy

For something simple like the DAS, it was not difficult to identify a meaningful sequence to build and integrate the pieces. However, generally there are a number of considerations that drive a good strategy. Things you want to think about as you're developing your strategy include:

- Incremental Development
- Priorities
- Major Risks

Incremental Development

First, as we've seen, you want to create something meaningful early and then incrementally build up the product functionality. So frequently you can identify what is most basic about your deliverable, create this, and then add complexity. For example, in a software product, there are frequently a few features that are used most of the time, and a number of features that are used occasionally. Here you would consider developing the frequently used features first, and then add the lesser used features. If you're not sure, look at use cases or scenarios: What will users be doing most of the time?

In some cases you may need to create a framework before you can add user functionality. Then you should first create something that is useful for the development team to build on. Something that will provide a common platform and makes test and integration easier. Then, individuals do not have to waste time creating their own unique test environment. And they can catch many integration issues before they start on the formal integration stage. In either case, creating something meaningful early is a great team motivator – they see that they are working on something real.

Priorities

Your strategy should reflect customer priorities. Identify the most important features and do these as early as possible. For example, if Marketing needs a prototype to demonstrate at a show, ask what differentiates your product from the competitors. These features have high priority and must be in the prototype. With a hard deadline you have to do things right. Projects struggle when they are near a promised delivery date and what's been done so far is not what the customer really needs.

Major Risks

The strategy is also where you address your major risks. For example, if you're not sure if it's possible to meet a requirement, you may need a quick assessment of how serious this is. You don't want a major surprise later. Here you might create a prototype to assess the requirement as early as possible. A limited functionality prototype is an effective way to test something that is high risk, and it gives you something that works sooner.

High risk deliverables might also interfere with the work of others on the team if they need to integrate with it to complete their work. A limited functionality prototype can also be useful here. For example, if there is a potential performance issue, the prototype can include the most useful functionality while ignoring the performance requirements. Then, with the prototype working the performance can be improved. Others can work with the prototype.

Developing a Strategy is Iterative

You start to lay out your strategy when you have a reasonably mature PBS. As you learn more about your project, you will add deliverables and stages, break up deliverables, and move deliverables around between stages. For example, you don't want to hold up integration while waiting for one deliverable. If one piece takes a lot longer than the others, consider breaking it up, moving it to a later stage, or completely changing that aspect of the strategy.

Sometimes risk, priority and durations will present competing demands. If this is the case, you might spend quite a bit of time iterating on your strategy to find a reasonable compromise. This might even continue into execution where problems and issues can force you to re-do your strategy.

How might the DAS strategy evolve?

The DAS strategy in Figure 6.1 is just a first pass. This will change as you learn more about the project, so let's look at how it might change.

Consider the special calculations that are integrated in Stage 3. Some issues you might have to deal with include: you need a specific resource who will start late, the complexity might present a schedule risk, or the complex temperature and pressure calculations might be very slow. You can address each of these in the strategy:

- If the resource is late, you might move the special calculations into Stage 4, or you might break it up and do some in Stage 3 and the rest in Stage 4. You might even add a stage between 3 and 4 just for the special calculations.
- To deal with the schedule risk due to complexity, you can prioritize the specific calculations, do the highest priority first and integrate whatever is complete by the time the other resources are ready to start Stage 3. Then you can integrate the remaining calculations when they are available or during Stage 4.
- Performance issues, such as complex calculations being too slow, are best handled by getting something working as soon as possible, integrating it in Stage 2, and then systematically improving performance. If possible, highlight the performance risk and use it to try to get the resource early.

Similarly, the Standard Routines might take too long to be in Stage 2. Since these are just a loose collection of useful routines, you can break them into two deliverables and do the first in Stage 2 and the second in Stage 3. You have to coordinate with those who need the routines so that they have what they need when they need it. If some of these routines are simple enough, you can also try to get a junior resource to help.

Unfortunately, I know of no tools for creating a strategy, so I just use Visio. Sometimes there is a lot of work updating dates and resources and moving things around, but I find the value it provides in understanding the project, in creating a close knit project team, and in communicating the big picture, is well worth the effort. Also, with Visio I can color code the deliverable by the group or resource responsible for each so everybody can tell at a glance where they fit in and who they have to interface with.

Managing the Project

Although this is a book about planning, it's important to point out that the strategy is also the tool you use for managing your project; the schedule is primarily for tracking progress. When things are not going according to plan, step back and assess the impact on the long term – the strategy. Is the problem big enough that you have to redo your strategy? This is important because if you try to assess the impact using the schedule, you can get lost in the details. Then you do things that seem right, but actually cause you to move away from your long term goals. Project managers who lose sight of, or fail to manage the big picture eventually lose control of their projects.

When managing the project, focus on the start dates for the near term milestones. Those contributing to these milestones must complete their deliverables on time. So you need to specifically ask if they will be finished in time to start the integration. That is, ask when they will be done, rather than for percent complete. If you know early enough that somebody cannot make it, you can usually plan a work around to minimize the impact to the overall schedule.

When problems necessitate a major update to the project plan, start with the strategy. Don't change the schedule until after you've updated the strategy. When you go directly to the schedule, with hundreds of tasks it's easy to miss opportunities. For example, it might be best for you to redefine one or more stages, or pull in the date of an unrelated deliverable to keep the project moving. You won't see this looking at the schedule.

When you complete an early stage that is a good time to stop and assess the overall status of your project. If you do this when you're approximately 25% complete with the project you will have a meaningful assessment, and enough time left to make changes if necessary. Compare your actual progress with your original plan to see how well you are doing. For example, suppose the DAS plan predicted stage 2 to be complete after two months but it actually took two and a half months, that is 25% longer. Then you can assume that if you continue with the current plan, the entire project will also take 25% longer. What was planned to be 8 months will likely take about 10 months. That is, unless you do something different.

Resist the temptation to say that because Stage 2 is two weeks behind, the entire project is two weeks behind. Rather, look at the causes for the slips and assess what you can do differently to avoid more slips. You might have to add resources, reduce functionality, or redo your strategy. Unless you make some changes, you will continue to slip.

The Project Crunch

Some project managers do not take advantage of incremental development, preferring to create all of the pieces in the PBS first and integrate them all together at the end. This approach, which I like to call the Big Bang, usually ends in what is commonly called the "project crunch". The project seems to move along reasonably well until it's time to start integrating the pieces together. Then, realizing that there is too much work and not enough time, everybody goes into "crunch" mode, working at 150 or 200% of capacity. This can go on for months, and go way past the scheduled end date of the project.

With a large number of pieces to integrate, many problems will be found and fixing one can cause problems elsewhere. Integration becomes unmanageable, and there is no way to predict when it will end. People can put in super-human efforts for short periods, but when they continue, both efficiency and effectiveness go down – you get less in 80 hours of work than you would have in 40 hours. And, the quality of what is produced is drastically reduced. In the end the project and the final product suffer.

A good strategy will not eliminate the project crunch, but will distribute it over the integration stages. At the end of each stage you have what might be called a "mini-crunch". The integration will not go as smoothly as planned. However, there are fewer pieces to integrate and there will be fewer problems during integration. Then there is more control over the integration, and the team will work a bit harder for a shorter period of time. When the integration is done the developers go back to a normal pace.

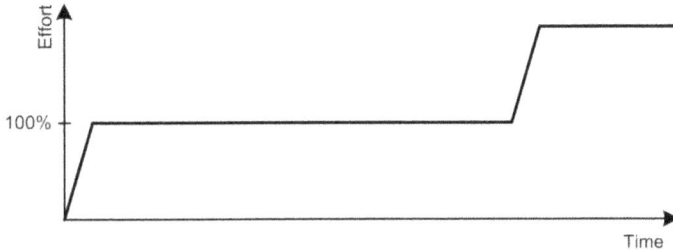

Figure 6.2a. The "Project Crunch"

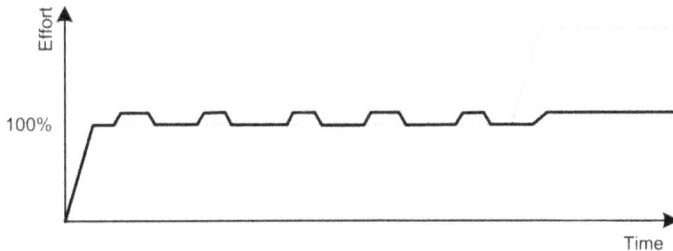

Figure 6.2b. A good strategy results in a number of mini-crunches.

You should also begin system testing as soon as you get to a stage with meaningful functionality. With a well thought out strategy this should be early rather than late in the development. Then you will identify many problems early and it will be easier to fix them.

Constant testing of the evolving product assures that when you get to formal system test there will be far fewer defects. You might have another mini-crunch, but, if system test was planned to take weeks, it should not take months, as it might when using the big bang approach.

Thus a good strategy not only creates a more manageable project, it also helps to ensure the quality of the final product. Problems are quickly discovered and easier to resolve. The project team doesn't get stressed out so they make a lot fewer mistakes.

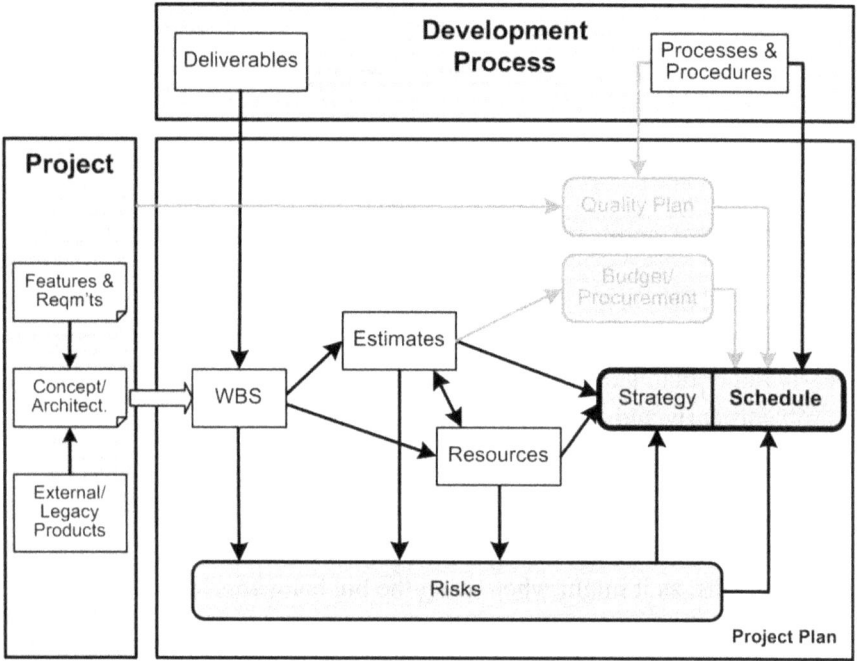

Development Process

Deliverables

Processes & Procedures

Project

Features & Reqm'ts

Concept/ Architect.

External/ Legacy Products

Quality Plan

Budget/ Procurement

WBS

Estimates

Resources

Strategy

Schedule

Risks

Project Plan

7 Pulling it Together: Your Schedule

Now we get the focus of planning – the schedule. The schedule is where we put all of the pieces together to establish the dates for tasks and milestones. First the WBS is transformed into an indented list and tasks are added:

- To create each deliverable
- To address risk, quality and procurement
- To support setting up hardware or a test system
- Etc.

Then estimates are made for each task, resources are assigned to them and predecessors are set based on the strategy and on resource needs.

If you have assigned owners to the WBS then the resources are easily filled in. For most tasks the owner will be the assigned resource. For a few there may be other resources assigned to assist the owner. Tasks like reviews and integration will have multiple resources assigned but there will be only one owner.

Each task will require an estimate, and the rollup of these estimates should be consistent with the earlier estimates for the deliverable. Typically, there will be differences because the tasks are estimated with finer granularity, and many little things overlooked in the high level estimates will be included. If there is a major difference you need to understand why.

Building the schedule is highly iterative. You will go through multiple passes adding tasks, switching resources and moving around the predecessors. In fact, the schedule is one thing you never really finish until the project is complete.

Typically, I start on my schedule before I've finished my WBS. Initially I focus on one owner, selecting the assigned deliverables and setting the information for their tasks. Then I move on to another owner. As I start getting realistic dates, I may update the strategy, rework the resource assignments or go back and redo some of my initial work. It's a lot of work but it is essential. The schedule is the most important part of your plan.

Work and Duration in the Schedule

When discussing estimates, we pointed out the difference between work and duration. Now this must be reflected in your schedule. You should enter work and percent availability for each resource, and let the scheduling software calculate duration. If a resource has estimated that a task will take one week, 40 hours, and the resource is available 100%, then when you enter 40 hours of work, the duration should be set to 5 days since 100% is generally the default availability. However, if you make the availability 50%, the resource will only work half time and the scheduling software will make the duration 10 days.

Discuss availability with each resource as you are gathering the estimates, and track it during project execution. It's not uncommon to have your resources support customers or other projects. When this happens, update the availability in the schedule so you can estimate the impact on project dates. Then report the new dates to your management.

Setting Predecessors

There are many reasons to set specific links in your schedule. Normally, there is a logical sequence in which tasks have to be performed. These I like to call hard dependencies. For example, you have to mix cement before you can pour it; you have to write software before you test it. Frequently, the tasks under the lowest level deliverables in your WBS all have a well defined logical sequence.

There are also soft dependencies where the order is not mandatory, but there is a good reason to perform tasks in a specific order. When you create your strategy you are defining a logical sequence. For example, with the DAS most of the data processing deliverables have no predefined sequence, but it was determined that the standard calculations should be created and integrated before the special calculations. This was to have the end-to-end data acquisition working as early as possible.

Another reason for setting order is risk. It's a good idea to address risk as early as possible. You want to know the seriousness as soon as possible and you want to prevent surprises at the end of the project. The major risks are addressed in your strategy, so now other risks you've identified should be considered when you're putting together the schedule.

Meeting the needs of other people can also set the sequence in which tasks are performed. One resource may need a specific deliverable from another resource to do his work. Recall that Joe wanted the raw data display to make his development easier.

Priority should also drive order. Like risk, priority should be considered in your strategy. You don't want to come up to a deadline with mostly low priority requirements completed. It's part of the project manager's responsibility to prevent this.

Predecessors are what ultimately take a task list and make it into a schedule. So take the time to think about setting those predecessors. It's your project, therefore it's your schedule.

Milestones

In addition to all of the tasks, you should have milestones liberally spread throughout your schedule. They allow you to track progress and to inform stakeholders of the important dates.

Your organization might define standard milestones such as:

- Specific reviews – e.g. for key documents such as Requirements
- The start or end of a project phase
- Alpha and Beta deliverables
- First customer ship
- Etc.

There are also Project Specific milestones that you define, such as:

- Stages of the strategy – start dates are used internally and end dates are reported outside of the project
- Key deliverables in the WBS
- External events – e.g. anything that drives your schedules such as the start of a resource or the delivery of essential equipment

Milestones are an important way for you to step back from the details in your schedule to see what you, as project manager, have to manage.

Creating the Schedule

Now you have to pull this together into a schedule. Figure 7.1 shows several sections of the DAS schedule. On top is the DAS Design Document. Joe is the assigned resource since he is the owner of the DAS. First Joe must develop the document. Tasks 3-6 list the technical sections and tasks 7-10 are standard process tasks to release, review, update and baseline the document. These standard process tasks are repeated for all documents, although the duration for review and update will depend on the size and complexity of the document. Tasks 7 and 10 are milestones to mark when the document is finished and when it is baselined.

Most of the predecessors are sequential. This is typical for a properly laid out schedule. Unfortunately, it's the non-sequential predecessors that represent most of the work of setting predecessors.

Below the design document are some of Joe's tasks to develop the DAS Interface software. Notice, there are two tasks under input simulator. Setting up the input simulator are examples of support tasks that were not identified in the WBS. Joe is assigned since he needs the simulator to test his software. Also notice that tasks 21 and 26 have multiple predecessors. Task 21 requires both the design document and the interface document (not shown) to be complete; task 26 is dependent on the task preceding it and task 95, which is the raw data display (not shown). Cliff is responsible for all of the displays, and Joe worked with Cliff to have this display early so he could use it to do his testing. The input simulator also needs to be a predecessor for task 26, but because the simulator was added after all of Joe's other work had been laid out, this was overlooked. It's common to overlook links on the first pass of a schedule and we'll address this shortly.

Under System Integration, tasks 140-147, are the first three stages of the strategy. You can see each stage has a large number of predecessors which are the completed deliverables needed for integration. Following this, at the very bottom, are the functional and system test tasks to test the completed software. You can see that the predecessors of the functional tests are the integration stages. Because the integration is being done incrementally, the functional test can also be incremental. That is, it starts before the software is complete. This helps to pull in the end date and assures a higher quality deliverable.

ID	Task Name	Durat.	Start	Finish	Predecess.	Res.
1	**Data Acquisition**	**52 days**	**1-Feb**	**12-Apr**		
2	**DAS Design Document**	**11 days**	**1-Feb**	**15-Feb**		
3	DAS Interface	3 days	1-Feb	3-Feb		Joe
4	Sensor List	2 days	6-Feb	7-Feb	3	Joe
5	Raw Data Acquisition	1 day	8-Feb	8-Feb	4	Joe
6	Calibration	1 day	9-Feb	9-Feb	5	Joe
7	DAS Document Release	0 days	9-Feb	9-Feb	6	Joe
8	DAS Document Review	2 days	10-Feb	13-Feb	7	Joe
9	DAS Document Update	1 day	14-Feb	14-Feb	8	Joe
10	Baseline DAS Document	0 days	14-Feb	14-Feb	9	Joe
	• • •					
19	**DAS Development**	**31 days**	**29-Feb**	**11-Apr**		
20	**DAS Interface Development**	**10 days**	**29-Feb**	**13-Mar**		
21	DAS Initialization and Setup	5 days	29-Feb	6-Mar	10,18	Joe
22	DAS Status	5 days	7-Mar	13-Mar	21	Joe
23	**Get Raw Data**	**8 days**	**14-Mar**	**23-Mar**		
24	Acquire Data	4 days	14-Mar	19-Mar	22	Joe
25	Store Data	2 days	20-Mar	21-Mar	24	Joe
26	Test Acquisition & Storage	2 days	22-Mar	23-Mar	25,95	Joe
27	**Input Simulator**	**3 days**	**26-Mar**	**28-Mar**		
28	Setup Voltage Simulator	2 days	26-Mar	27-Mar	26	Joe
29	Test Simulator Output	1 day	28-Mar	28-Mar	28	Joe
	• • •					
140	**System Integration**	**65 days**	**1-Feb**	**1-May**		
141	Integration Plan	5 days	1-Feb	7-Feb		PM
142	**Stage 1: Basic Data Acquisition**	**3 days**	**26-Mar**	**28-Mar**		
143	Stage 1: Basic Data Acquisition	3 days	26-Mar	28-Mar	141,22,26, 95	Joe
144	**Stage 2: Full Data Acquisition**	**5 days**	**5-Apr**	**11-Apr**		
145	Stage 2: Full Data Acquisition	5 days	5-Apr	11-Apr	142,34,56, 61,74,99	Joe
146	**Stage 3: Special Data Calculation**	**5 days**	**18-Apr**			
147	Stage 3: Special Data Calculatio	5 days	18-Apr	24-Apr	143,66,94, 77,103, 107, 130	Amy
	• • •					
159	**Functional Test**	**21 day**	**12-Apr**	**11-May**		
160	Data Acquisition	5 days	12-Apr	18-Apr	158,145	Hank
161	Data Processing	5 days	25-Apr	1-May	160,147	Hank
162	Data Display	5 days	2-May	8-May	161,151	Hank
163	Data Archive	3 days	9-May	11-May	162,149	Hank
164	**Systems Test**	**17 days**	**14-May**	**5-Jun**		
165	User Scenarios	10 days	14-May	25-May	163	Hank
166	Fault Conditions	7 days	28-May	5-Jun	165	Hank

Figure 7.1. Selected tasks from the DAS Schedule.

Gantt Chart

The Gantt chart shows the time sequence of the tasks in the project, with a bar from the start to the finish of each task. For many people, this is what they mean by a schedule. It's easy to see the timing of all tasks, and possibly the inter-relationships between tasks. When you have to share the schedule with others, it's usually in the form of a Gantt chart.

On the next page we have a section from the DAS software Gantt. The list of tasks is on the left side. Here we have some of Joe's tasks during the first seven weeks of the project. This task list includes only the ID and task name, but you can include any task information that you think is important.

The time bars are on the right. Across the top is the timeline which is marked off in weekly increments. I recommend that you choose an increment that is appropriate for your project. Weekly is good for a project of a few months, but when it gets to a year or more, switch it to monthly.

Below the timeline are the schedule bars. The dark grey bars are for summary tasks – they show the total time span for all of the tasks under that summary task. The shaded bars below the summary tasks are for the individual tasks. To the right is the name of the resource assigned to the task. You can see for the two document reviews that the entire team is assigned. Finally, the diamonds are for milestones. For each document there is a milestone when the document is released for review and another when it is baselined.

One thing not shown here is that scheduling software can also show the critical path by making those bars red. We'll talk about the critical path shortly, and when you have to pull in a schedule, this is where you start.

Many people prefer this graphical format to a table with a list of dates and names, or to a summary list of milestones. However, they can get difficult to read. I've had to print them on multiple sheets of plotter paper, each 4 feet wide by 3 feet high.

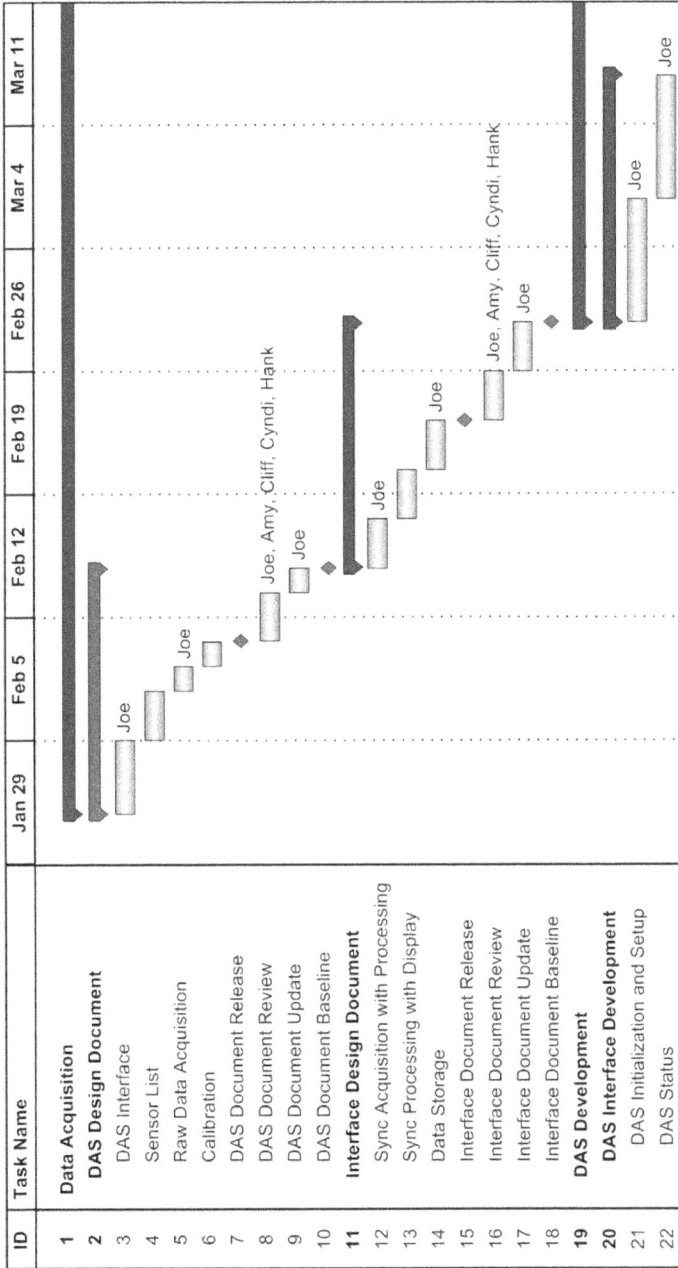

Figure 7.2. A section of the DAS Gantt Chart.

Network Diagram

Another schedule view of importance is the network diagram. This was called a PERT Chart and some people still use that terminology. The network diagram shows the logical relationships between tasks.

Here we have a small section of the network diagram for the DAS software. Most of the tasks just proceed in a sequence. These represent the work of the individual contributors. There are also inter-task links, such as the deliverables that feed into each stage of the strategy. Some of these links shown here are:

- Tasks 22, 26 and 94 link to the Stage 1 integration
- Tasks 56, 95 and 130 link to Stage 2 (that task is not shown)
- Task 94 is linked to task 26 so Joe can use the raw data display

Other useful information on this segment of the diagram includes:

- Tasks 142, 28 and 31 are being done in parallel. Joe is responsible for these and this is why he is overloaded.
- Tasks 28 and 29, the simulator tasks that were added and then assigned to Joe, are dangling – there is no successor. This you would fix when you level Joe's work.

The network diagram is more useful than the Gantt chart when you're working on the logic in the schedule. Leaving out just a few key links can cause problems that are not detected until it's too late to fix them. Here you can trace the tasks of individual resources, see where they are doing tasks in parallel, and mark up the network diagram to resolve the overallocation.

The network diagram is also a great team building tool. People can see the flow of the project and identify interim products that might be useful to them. We know that Joe has requested the raw data display. Cliff, who is doing the displays, might request the temperature and pressure drop calculations (tasks 59 and 60) so he can use them for his Subsystem 2 Display (task 98). Similarly, Cyndi might request all of the unit conversion software which is completed after task 57, so she can add them to the 1-minute trend updates (task 133).

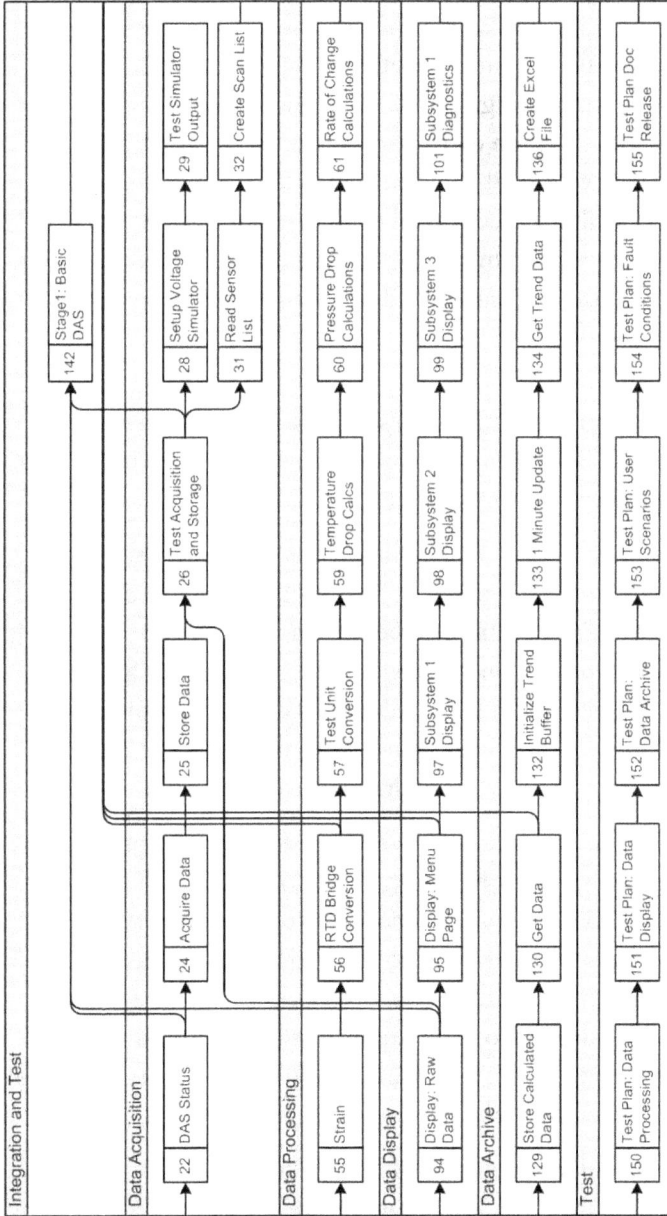

Figure 7.3. A section of the DAS Network Diagram

On one project to develop a large electro-mechanical system, I was able to use a network diagram to help integrate engineering and manufacturing. The manufacturing group reviewed the engineering tasks to identify those that produced an output that would be useful for manufacturing. For example, with a preliminary design of the mechanical frame, manufacturing was able to get an early start on the design of the electrical harnesses that snake the electrical signals through the frame. They also worked more closely with the mechanical engineers designing the frame, and were able to suggest design modifications to make wire routing easier. The result was reduced time to market and lower manufacturing costs.

Critical Path

The critical path is the longest path in the schedule. It determines the duration of your project. A task is on the critical path if a delay in the start or finish will cause the end date to slip.

Consider a simple project with just three tasks. Tasks 1 and 3 each take 5 days, and task 2 takes 3 days. In addition, Tasks 1 and 2 can be done in parallel, but they both must be complete before Task 3 can start. The Gantt chart will look like Figure 7.4a on the next page. Tasks 1 and 3 are on the critical path. At five days each, it will take you 10 days to complete the project. If either of them takes longer than 5 days, or if either of them is delayed, then the project will take more than 10 days.

Task 2 starts at the same time as task 1, but has a shorter duration, so it is not on the critical path. In fact, it has 2 days slack, meaning that the finish date can slip by up to 2 days before it impacts the critical path. And if it did slip by 2 days, then Task 2 would move to the critical path (Figure 7.4b). Similarly, if the duration was increased to 5 days, or there was a one day slip and an increase in duration to 4 days, then Task 2 would also move to the critical path. In the figure we show what would happen if the start date slips by 2 days. All three tasks would be on the critical path.

Now suppose that in addition to the two day slip, the duration of Task 2 increases to 4 days (Figure 7.4c). Then, the start of Task 3 is pushed out by a day, and the schedule slips. But, if Task 1 remains at 5 days, then it is no longer on the critical path, since it can slip by one day or take 6 days to

Task 1	5 days	
Task 2	3 days	
Task 3		5 days

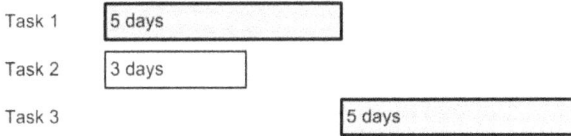

Figure 7.4a. A simple schedule highlighting the Critical Path.

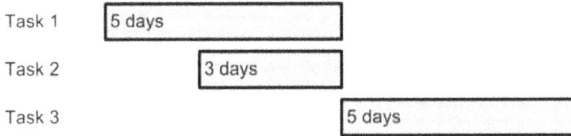

Task 1	5 days	
Task 2		3 days
Task 3		5 days

Figure 7.4b. When Task 2 slips, it becomes on the Critical Path.

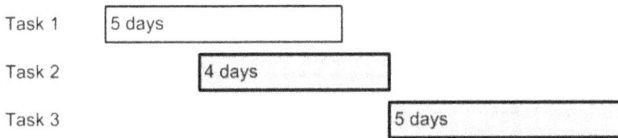

Task 1	5 days	
Task 2		4 days
Task 3		5 days

Figure 7.4c. When Task 2 takes longer it pushes out the end date.

complete without impacting the end date. So as you're tracking your schedule you have to frequently reassess the critical path to prevent surprises. You don't want a task that you think is not on the critical path, to slip, move to the critical path and then push out the end date before you realize you have a problem.

Scheduling tools calculate a parameter called total slack or total float which tells how far off the critical path a non-critical task is. Based on the duration of your project you might want to flag all tasks with a total slack less than a few days or even a few weeks as being on the critical path to prevent surprises. In Microsoft Project you can set tasks to be on the critical path if the total slack is less than a specific value. For a 6 month project I'll set this to 5 days, and if the project is more than a year, I'll increase it to 10 days.

As you're assessing the critical path look at the resources assigned the tasks. These resources will drive you project. Determine if they:

- Have the skills and skill level required
- Are supporting other projects
- Have a history of coming in early, on time or late

Resource Utilization

Once you have completed a first pass off your schedule, Review all of the assignments to check if the work is evenly distributed and if any of the resources are overloaded.

The table below is similar to a resource utilization table you might see in your scheduling software. Here it is on a monthly basis to look at the big picture. Also, the allocation is in percent, which is easier to interpret then hours, because the total number of hours vary from month-to-month.

Name	Group	Work	Feb	Mar	Apr	May	Jun
Joe	Acquisition	584 hrs	124%	127%	90%		
Amy	Processing	560 hrs	133%	100%	95%		
Cyndi	Archive	312 hrs	138%	32%	14%		
Cliff	Display	512 hrs	133%	100%	62%	4%	
Hank	Test	600 hrs	48%	100%	81%	100%	14%
PM		40 hrs	24%				

Table 7.1. Example of a Resource Utilization table.

This brief table contains quite a bit of useful information:

- The work is not evenly distributed
- Joe is assigned the most work
- Cyndi has much less work than the others
- Most resources are overallocated in February
- Joe is also overallocated in March

Dealing with the uneven work distribution is a project specific challenge. Here, all of the resources are specialists so it's not possible to just reassign tasks. Each task must be assigned to somebody who can do it. Therefore you need to work with your team to identify possible solutions. They can propose work reassignment that you might not think of, and there will be buy-in by the team when they're done.

Start the discussion by pointing out the current status: Joe has too much work and Cyndi has a lot less than the others. Then ask Joe what he could possibly give up and ask Cyndi what other tasks she might be able to do. In this case, what you are likely to hear is that Joe does not have to do the interface document which details the interfaces between acquisition and processing, and between processing and display. Since Amy is responsible for all of the processing, she could create it. However, Amy also has a lot of work and it's not feasible to give her an additional 80 hours unless some of her other work can be transferred to another resource. Here Cyndi might volunteer to help Amy by doing some of the calculations. She has some experience and can do the unit conversion calculations (32 hours), some of the standard routines (40 hours) and she can take over the Stage 3 integration (40 hours). So Cyndi can take 112 hours of work from Amy, and she thinks she can do it in about the same amount of time. This allows Amy to do the interface document, taking 80 hours from Joe.

Tasks are still not perfectly distributed, but Joe and Amy have reduced their work. Joe, Amy and Cliff have around 500 hours, and Cyndi has over 400. A significantly improved distribution.

Unfortunately, in the schedule there is more to do than just change resource names. Many of the predecessors will change, and this is the most difficult part. Consider, when Joe was responsible for acquisition and the interface documents, he started his development work when both were complete. His early work on the DAS interface and gathering raw data does not depend on the Interface document. So these can start after he has completed the design document. He will need the acquisition to processing portion of the interface document when he stores the data he has gathered. Similarly, for Cyndi's processing tasks she only needs the design document. She does not need any of Amy's development. So you can see it can be quite a bit of work moving the assignments around.

While you're doing this you also have to deal with the overallocation. In February all of the resources are reviewing documents at the same time as they are doing their own assigned work. And Joe's overallocation in March is caused by multiple tasks being performed in parallel. Joe is responsible for Stages 1 and 2 of the integration and the tasks to create the input simulator. These are scheduled to occur while he is working on other development tasks. Overallocation issues like this are not uncommon, and we'll discuss how to level resources shortly. However, it's important to note that leveling the resources will frequently push out the dates, so you have to do this before you commit to any dates!

As you're moving tasks and assignments around take your time and think about it. If not, you will have to do it over and over.

Resource Leveling

As you are putting together your schedule, it's inevitable that a few resources will become over allocated – they are scheduled to work on two or more tasks at the same time. We saw this when we looked at the resource utilization. Everybody was overloaded in February because of the document reviews, and Joe was also overloaded because he was expected to work on three different tasks at the same time. Let's look at one of Joe's overallocations first.

Two of the tasks Joe is working on parallel are: task 31: Read the Sensor List and task 142: Stage 1 Integration. Figure 7.5a (opposite) shows how the Gantt chart might look for these tasks. Let's see how to deal with it.

The easiest way to resolve an overallocation is to assign another resource to one or more of the tasks. To do this you must have a resource who is both available and capable of doing the work. If you have a lot of tasks that are fairly routine or not too difficult then see if you can get a junior resource to help out.

Reassigning tasks is not always an option, so frequently you will serialize the tasks. Here you have to decide which task should be done first, and identify what links have to change and how they should change. I find that marking up a network diagram of the specific person's tasks is the best way to quickly identify the links that have to be changed. In Figure 7.5b it is assumed that the integration is more important so it is done first, and the appropriate serialization is shown. There are other links to consider. For example, Stage 2 is a successor to Stage 1. When you make task 31 a successor to Stage 1, you have to consider if you have to make it a predecessor to Stage 2 also. Here, because Joe has tasks that come after task 31 and are also predecessors to Stage 2, this will not be necessary.

Finally, Joe can split his time on each task, as shown in Figure 7.5c. Some people like to work this way – when they're stuck on one task they switch over to the other and give their brain a break. I will put it in the schedule like this to balance out their workload, and then let them manage how they actually split their time. I only insist that they not miss a major milestone.

31	Read Sensor List	2 days	Joe
32	Create Scan List	2 days	Joe
142	Stage 1: Integration	3 days	Joe

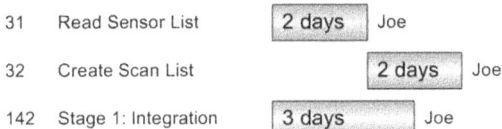

Figure 7.5a. Joe is overallocated.

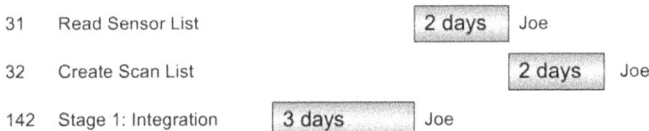

31	Read Sensor List	2 days	Joe
32	Create Scan List	2 days	Joe
142	Stage 1: Integration	3 days	Joe

Figure 7.5b. Resolving the overallocation by serializing the tasks.

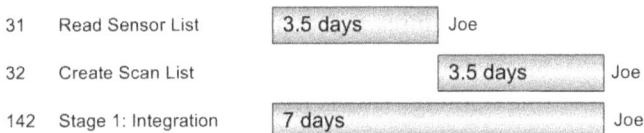

31	Read Sensor List	3.5 days	Joe
32	Create Scan List	3.5 days	Joe
142	Stage 1: Integration	7 days	Joe

Figure 7.5c. Resolving the overallocation by splitting Joe's time.

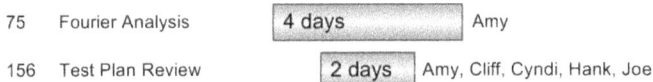

| 75 | Fourier Analysis | 4 days | Amy |
| 156 | Test Plan Review | 2 days | Amy, Cliff, Cyndi, Hank, Joe |

Figure 7.5d. Amy's overallocation because of a design review

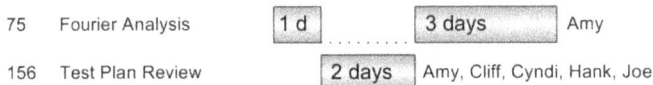

| 75 | Fourier Analysis | 1 d | 3 days | Amy |
| 156 | Test Plan Review | 2 days | Amy, Cliff, Cyndi, Hank, Joe |

Figure 7.5e. Software leveling splits Task 75 to resolve the overallocation.

Sometimes a resource has to stop working on one task, perform another, and then complete the first – e.g. a document must be reviewed when it becomes available. To do this, the first task must be split up. Figure 7.5d shows that Amy must review the Test Plan while she is scheduled to work on the Fourier Calculations. By setting Task 156 to a higher priority, using the leveling in your scheduling tool will split Task 75 to level Amy's work, as shown in Figure 7.5e. I strongly recommend you do as much manual leveling as possible before using software leveling. When you do the leveling, you make the choices. When the software does the leveling, the choices may be arbitrary. Also, when you do the leveling by setting predecessors and successors, this preserves the critical path.

Nonworking Time

When you're dealing with your resources, don't forget to add nonworking time, such as holidays and vacations to your calendars. Nonworking time will push out the end date of the schedule and you must make sure you have this in the schedule as soon as possible. Next we will consider pulling in the schedule, and you don't want to do that, get a more acceptable date, and then realize you have to add vacations and holidays.

Training will also add time to your schedule, so don't forget it. Get time estimates from those taking the training and consider if, when they return, they will have to then train others on the project. Also consider if there will be a learning curve after the training. This is frequently the case when you're dealing with complex hardware or software.

Pulling in the Critical Path

When you have your schedule leveled, it's almost guaranteed that you'll be asked to pull it in. The place to start is the critical path. If you can shorten the critical path, you can pull in the end date. However, you might not be able to pull it in by too much. That's because, as you shorten the critical path you are also reducing the total slack for the tasks that are not on the critical path. Eventually, tasks that had just a few days total slack will create a new critical path. So it's an iterative process. Periodically you have to stop, reassess what is on the critical path, and see if you can continue to reduce the new critical path.

The first thing you should do is try to add resources. If your management is dictating the schedule finish date, then they should provide the necessary resources to do the work. From your analysis of the critical path, you know where you could add a resource, how much work there is, and what are the consequences if you cannot get them. You have to be prepared to argue your case and be persistent. Keep pointing out the consequences – what it is that they want that they will not be able to get. Also consider eliminating features or deliverables. You have to be specific:

- What do you want to eliminate?

- What will it buy you?
- What is the impact on the final product?
- When can it be delivered?

Again, you have to be prepared to answer questions.

Sometimes you can move resources around. From your assessment and from the resource usage table, you should know:

- Who is not on the critical path and who might be available?
- How much time do they have?
- What can they do?
- And, where can they help those on the critical path?

Also, review the predecessor/successor logic you have set. Are there tasks in series that could be done in parallel? These would have to be tasks done by different resources, where the resource responsible for the successor task has enough slack to start early.

More frequently, you cannot do the tasks in parallel but the successor task can get started before the predecessor is finished. This is something you will have to manage to make sure that when the predecessor task is started, it first does what the successor needs to start. Recall, for example, when looking at resource utilization, trying to balance Joe's workload, he did not need the entire interface document, just the acquisition to processing portion. To satisfy Joe, Amy would have to do this portion first.

Doing tasks in parallel is known as fast tracking the schedule. You have to do a thorough analysis of the schedule to identify where you can loosen your predecessor requirements. Be forewarned that fast tracking can increase risk and you need to manage this risk. You'll be starting some tasks before all predecessors are fully available. So you have to coordinate between the resources doing the fast track tasks and those doing their predecessors. Everything has to flow smoothly. There's no room for errors.

Finally, you should also go back and review your estimates. People know more, and they might be able to reduce the duration of some tasks. However, it's just as likely that they identify more work and will increase others. Whatever you do, resist the temptation to pressure the resources to reduce their estimates. This will pull in the schedule date, but it will likely push out the real end date. We'll address this when we discuss quality, but people tend to make more mistakes when pressured to reduce the estimate, and the time gained up front will be lost in integration and testing.

An Example of pulling in the end date

On the next page, Figure 7.6a shows a network diagram containing eleven tasks. Currently the duration is 32 days, but you've been asked to pull it in. The critical path includes tasks 1, 2, 3, 4, and 11, which are highlighted. Clearly, the easiest way to pull in the schedule is to shorten Task 1 or Task 11 or both. Tasks 2, 3 and 4 are in parallel with the other tasks, so you can only pull in the end date by two days by shortening these tasks.

Discussing this with Cyndi, she says that even with 10 days Task 1 is going to be tight. She is also not comfortable reducing Task 11. However, she thinks she can reduce Task 4 to 6 days. Updating the schedule, Figure 7.6b, the duration is reduced to 30 days, but now both Cyndi and Joe are on the critical path. To reduce the schedule further you have to get creative.

Amy has a couple of days of slack, so you chat with Amy and Cyndi to see if Amy can help with Task 11. Since Task 11 is integrating all of the pieces, it could start early with Tasks 3, 5 and 8. Amy is responsible for Task 8, and she is familiar with 3 and 5, so she thinks she can integrate these three in 2 days. Then Cyndi will need 4 days for the rest of Task 11.

So, you split Task 11 in 11a and 11b, assign 11a to Amy, move it after Task 8, and add the links from Tasks 3 and 5 to Task 11a. This new schedule is shown in Figure 7.6c. Now you've pulled in the schedule from 32 to 28 days. But Cyndi, Joe and Amy are all on the critical path and Hank has only two days of slack. You have no contingency if problems arise. But this is what happens when you aggressively pull in a schedule.

One other thing you can do is to see if Joe, Amy and Hank can start before Cyndi finishes Task 1. You need to determine if Cyndi will have something she can share with them by the end of week 1. She may, but only if you ask her about it before hand. If you just ask her at the end of week 1, she is likely to say that what she has isn't in a form to share with others. Here you're proactively managing the schedule.

This example has only 11 tasks, but even with hundreds of tasks, it more complicated and also highly iterative. But the process is the same.

Task 1		Task 2		Task 3		Task 4		Task 11	
10d	Cyndi	4d	Cyndi	4d	Cyndi	8d	Cyndi	6d	Cyndi

Task 5		Task 6	
12d	Joe	2d	Joe

Task 7		Task 8	
11d	Amy	1d	Amy

Task 9		Task 10	
5d	Hank	5d	Hank

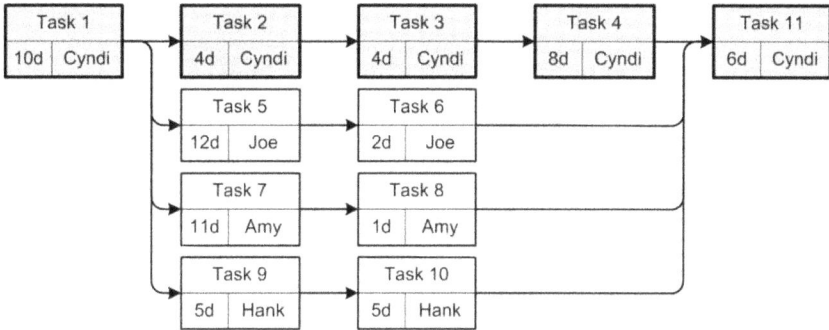

Figure 7.6a. A schedule that needs to be pulled in.

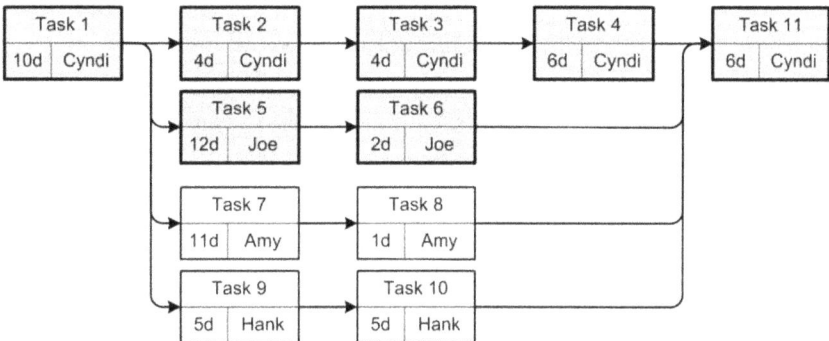

Task 1		Task 2		Task 3		Task 4		Task 11	
10d	Cyndi	4d	Cyndi	4d	Cyndi	6d	Cyndi	6d	Cyndi

Task 5		Task 6	
12d	Joe	2d	Joe

Task 7		Task 8	
11d	Amy	1d	Amy

Task 9		Task 10	
5d	Hank	5d	Hank

Figure 7.6b. Reducing Task 4 reduces the duration but puts Joe on the Critical Path.

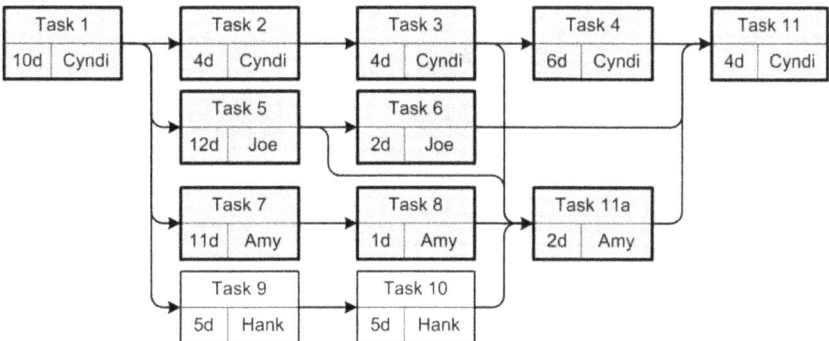

Task 1		Task 2		Task 3		Task 4		Task 11	
10d	Cyndi	4d	Cyndi	4d	Cyndi	6d	Cyndi	4d	Cyndi

Task 5		Task 6	
12d	Joe	2d	Joe

Task 7		Task 8		Task 11a	
11d	Amy	1d	Amy	2d	Amy

Task 9		Task 10	
5d	Hank	5d	Hank

Figure 7.6c. Splitting Task 11 between Cyndi and Amy reduces the duration more but adds Amy to the Critical Path.

Buffers

One way to deal with schedule risk is to add contingency. Buffers are a good way to add that contingency. Say your schedule says you'll be done at the end of May, but you really don't feel this is realistic. You know there is quite a bit of uncertainty on you major deliverable. However, it's important to keep your project team working to the schedule date, so you don't want to change it. What you can do is add a buffer to the end of the schedule. With a two week buffer, your committed delivery date is moved to the middle of June.

It's easy to create a buffer for a milestone:

1. Add another milestone and link it to the desired milestone
2. Add the desired buffer to the date of the original milestone date
3. Using this calculated date, set a must finish on date for the buffered (i.e. added) milestone

If the schedule end date is May 31 and you want to buffer this by two weeks, then fix the date on the buffered milestone to be June 14. Then, as you track your schedule, your end date might slip if the tasks driving it slip, but your buffered milestone will remain fixed. That is, as long as you do not slip more than two weeks during project execution.

You should periodically check the remaining buffer and estimate how fast it is changing. Say for example that you're 25% complete with your project and you've used up 50% of your buffer. Then, unless you do something radically different you're probably in trouble. You're going to run out of buffer before you run out of time. On the other hand, if your buffer has been reduced by 25% or less, then you are probably in good shape.

I try to add a buffer only to the end of my schedule. However, when you have an internal milestone that is very important you might want to buffer it. Typically this might be one of the milestones in your strategy where you have a partially working deliverable that others need.

Estimate the size of a buffer

With 3-point estimates, the range from the nominal to the worst case was considered a good measure of the seriousness of a risk. When the range was large we used scenarios to estimate the most likely duration. If, after

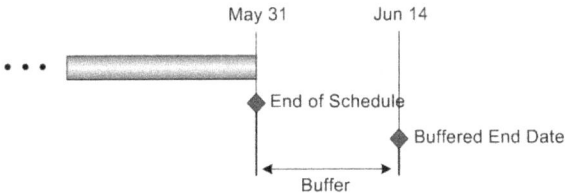

Figure 7.7a. Adding a buffer to the end of a task.

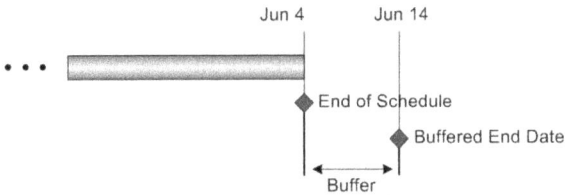

Figure 7.7b. The buffered end date is preserved when the task slips.

replacing the nominal with the most likely there is still a relatively large range, you might consider adding a buffer. There are statistical formulas, using PERT (i.e. 3-point) estimates which can estimate buffer size from the standard deviation of the three estimates. However, these are complex, and we can get reasonable estimates by just taking half the range:

$$\text{Range} = \text{Worst Case} - \text{Most Likely}$$

$$\text{Buffer} = \text{Range}/2$$

So, if the most likely estimate for a deliverable is six weeks and the worst-case is eight weeks, you should consider a one-week buffer. With this you should have better than 80% probability of hitting your target.

If you have two uncertain deliverables driving the same milestone, add the two ranges and divide by three:

$$\text{Buffer} = (\text{Range}_1 + \text{Range}_2)/3$$

There's no need to try to get too precise because what we have are only estimates of the true numbers. Also, as I calculate contingency or buffer size, I tend to round my numbers off to the nearest week anyway.

If you have more than two uncertain deliverables you should rethink your strategy, or update your estimates, rather than rely on buffers.

One Deliverable Driving Multiple Buffers

If you have multiple buffers in your schedule, you may have to deal with an uncertain deliverable that impacts two or more of these buffers. Consider a high level deliverable where, having estimated the range, you feel that there is still too much uncertainty so you want to add contingency to the schedule. Also assume that this deliverable was broken down, into two components, where the first component drives the internal milestone that you want to buffer, and the second component drives the end date, which you also want to buffer. Here you need to determine if the worst case duration is driven by the first component or the second. If the uncertainty is mostly in the first component, then use the range to size this internal buffer; if not, use the range to size the overall schedule buffer.

For example, if performance is both uncertain and critical, and you must meet the performance requirements when you complete the internal milestone, then the worst case will dive the internal buffer. However, if performance is not important for the internal milestone, e.g. you are just integrating some early deliverables, the worst case will drive the schedule buffer.

On rare occasions you may have to split the range between the two milestones. Here, don't try to be too precise, roughly estimate how much of the range drives the first buffer and use the remainder to drive the schedule buffer. The one thing you don't want to do is to use the total uncertainty to size each of the buffers. Then you will be adding contingency to deal with the uncertainty twice.

Baseline Your Schedule

Now, when you're finished with your schedule, or at least you think you're finished, set a baseline. A baseline is a reference point – your initial estimate of how the project should progress. By comparing what you've done to what you planned to do, you can make better predictions of the final schedule and cost.

Scheduling software like Microsoft Project has built in functions to create a baseline from the current schedule. These will save the start and finish dates and the duration for all tasks.

I also save a copy of this baselined schedule in a file where the file name is clearly labeled baseline, and includes the date of the baseline. As the execution of the project progresses, tasks are added, deleted and moved around. Having this file gives me a good way of comparing the initial schedule with an interim or the final schedule.

With the baseline, we've completed our schedule.

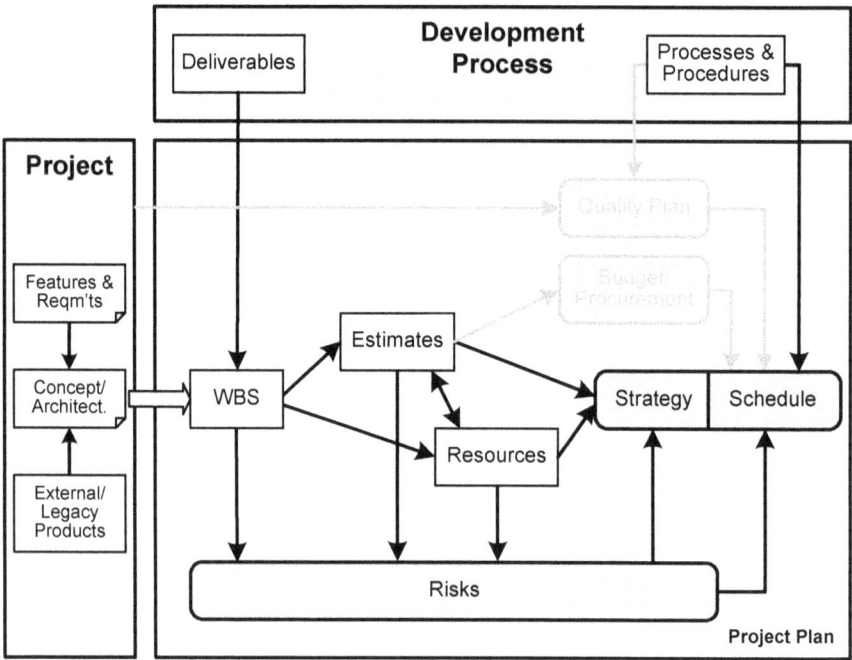

Development Process

Deliverables

Processes & Procedures

Project

Features & Reqm'ts

Concept/ Architect.

External/ Legacy Products

Quality Plan

Budget/ Procurement

WBS

Estimates

Resources

Strategy

Schedule

Risks

Project Plan

8 Iterate! Iterate! Iterate!

Planning is an iterative process. The early iterations help you to scope out your project, identify resource needs and start setting expectations. Early on, your primary focus is your schedule and its driving elements – WBS, risk, resources, etc. These are the elements we've discussed up to this point. However, early on you have limited project understanding, so the process you use is somewhat abbreviated from what we've presented. Therefore, at this point it's appropriate to stop and look at this abbreviated process. As you will see, your plan is actually something that evolves.

Recall when discussing estimates you create top-down, bottom-up, and finally detailed schedule estimates. The top-down estimates provide rough sizing information, and the bottom-up estimates provide the basis for your early plans.

Getting a meaningful assessment of schedule, resources and risk as early as possible is very important. While you will not commit to a preliminary plan, it does help to set expectations. For example, the resources allocated might not be sufficient to do the work within the desired timeframe. You may need to bargain for more resources or for different resources. Having a plan and some what-if scenarios will help you make your case especially when you can highlight the impact of inadequate resources.

If your organization uses a phase gate process, then you must create an early plan for the concept phase. The preliminary schedule, resource needs and major risks are used with the business case to decide whether to continue the project or not. Also, in an Agile environment, management might require a reasonable schedule estimate before the team can start on the iterations. In both cases you will have to generate a meaningful plan with just a partial PBS and early bottom-up estimates.

Planning is also a concurrent process. When you focus on a deliverable, think about who's going to do the work, how long it's going to take, what are the risks associated with it, and where does it best fit in to the strategy. These are all inter-related and if you deal with them separately you will miss something.

Starting Up the Project: Your First Iteration

Early on you will follow a reduced version of the planning process. Working with one or two senior people, a list of features and a concept, you will start to develop your PBS. With this you generate some bottom-up estimates, identify resources and the major risks, and then start thinking about how you might put it all together.

Now is the time to start thinking about risk and even addressing it in your early strategy. For example, if you feel you need a prototype, add it to the strategy and keep notes of why you need it. The notes will morph into your integration plan. Also start a risk log to capture the risks identified. And remember to ask about potential problems and worst case estimates.

Quality is mostly process, so you don't do much on your quality plan early on. However, if you know that you have stringent quality requirements, assess the risk and also determine if they should be reflected in the strategy. Similarly, you would only consider Budget in the first pass when you have major, long lead time purchases.

The first pass planning process flow is shown in Figure 8.1 on the next page. Below this are examples of an early PBS for the DAS (Figure 8.2) and an early a Strategy based on the PBS. The focus of the PBS is acquisition, processing and display, and these are not as detailed as in the final PBS (Figure 8.3). Data Archive is just a placeholder; at this point it is not believed to be important enough to dig down into it. With this PBS, the strategy has only three stages, and the last one just includes what is left over after the first two.

Now you can estimate the total project duration. Starting with the first stage, you know how long it will take to create each deliverable. You also know one person will do both the DAS Interface and the Sensor List so these must be done in series. With these you can calculate the duration before this stage can start. Similarly, for the other two stages, you have estimates for the deliverables and you know which can be done in parallel (different resources) and which in series (only one resource). Then you add the durations for the three stages and you have an estimate of how long the project will take. The duration is each stage is based on the longest duration driving that stage, so the number is a little conservative. However, since early estimates tend to be optimistic this approach is not unreal.

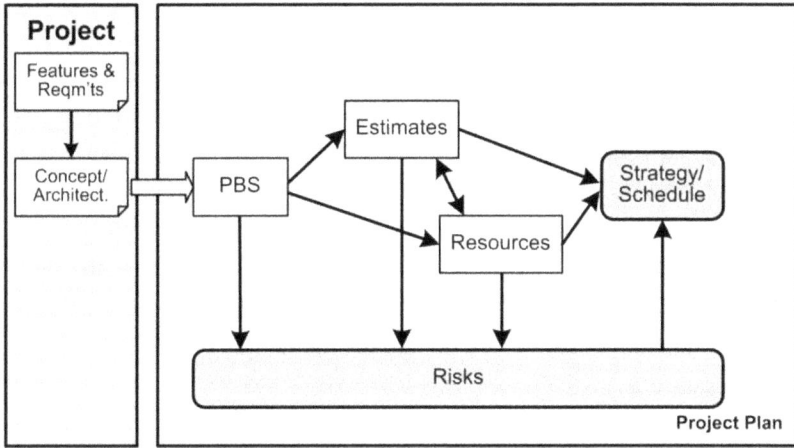

Figure 8.1. The planning process for the first iteration of your plan.

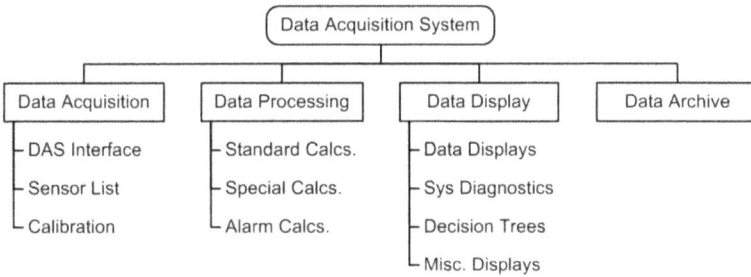

Figure 8.2. An early PBS.

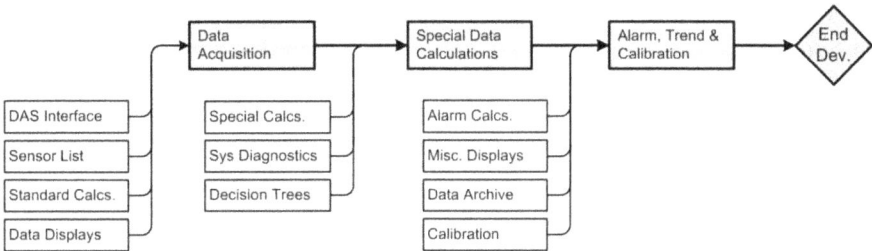

Figure 8.3. The early strategy based on the early PBS.

When you have historical data from past projects to drive these early estimates, you can make reasonable projections.

Your Second Iteration

With the first pass complete, you expand the PBS into the WBS. At this point, as you're gathering estimates, you should have at least the key resources assigned. They study the requirements, help formalize the concept or architecture, and may start some detailed design. Having frequent, informal chats with them as they are doing this can provide tremendous insight. Listen to their concerns and determine if they should be transformed into risks. Rollup the estimates to check if they are different from the initial top-down estimates. If so, identify why. If necessary, start resetting expectations.

Be in constant communications with your resources so you can see things as they evolve. It's fairly common for them to run into something unforeseen, and you can help assess the impact. They have different priorities and a different perspective than you. What is important to you might not seem important to them. So they might not see the need to report all issues.

If there is an external product or a legacy system associated with the project, now is the time to consider how much work or risk it will add to the project. If appropriate, add it to the WBS.

Also, if you have major procurement, identify items with long lead times and those where you might have difficulty getting the necessary funding. If other deliverables can't be finished or tested until these purchases are in-house, then the purchases need to be reflected in the strategy. The rough delivery dates will determine if they belong in early or late stages.

During this phase the information in the WBS is rapidly expanding so you will start capturing it in your scheduling software. Then the dates you assign to the strategy can come from this schedule and are a little more meaningful that the quick and dirty calculations used in the first phase.

If there is a big difference between this and your first estimates of scope, schedule and cost or resource needs, then open discussions of what you need and what you can do. Now, with a better understanding of the project you can be more specific, especially in the number of resources and the specific skills required. This is also a good time to identify the need for an

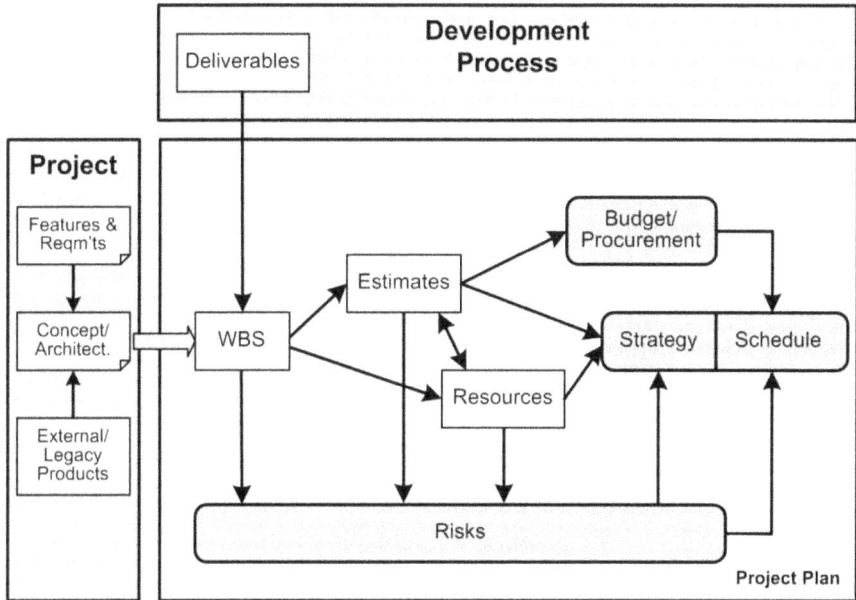

Figure 8.4. A typical planning process for your second iteration.

early prototype, or to determine if you need to break up a complex deliverable across multiple stages in the strategy. By the time you finish this stage, your strategy should be pretty solid. If there are no more major surprises then next you will primarily fill in the details in the schedule and make sure everybody understands the quality processes and how they will be applied to the project deliverables.

Finalizing Your Detailed Plan

Now your strategy is reasonably stable and you will spend a lot of time working on your schedule. Here you will invariably see problems. As they say, the devil's in the details! You will be able to look more closely at resource assignments, and there will be over allocated resources to level. As we saw when leveling the DAS schedule, much of this happens when you add the miscellaneous tasks and start assigning them to an appropriate resource They generally do not add a lot to the total work, but they can push out the schedule.

While not too common, when you expand the deliverable into specific tasks, additional work may be uncovered that will further push out your earlier estimates. If serious enough, you may have to renegotiate the project requirements to eliminate a problematic requirement. This is especially true if you have a fixed delivery date.

You should understand your quality needs as you go through your earlier iterations on the plan. But now you should be putting together your quality plan. As we'll see, quality is mostly process which translates to tasks that have to be added to the schedule. Recall that the DAS schedule had a number of tasks to perform design review, and update the documents. These tasks are the major elements in the DAS quality control plan. Testing is also part of quality control. Once you understand the quality processes, you automatically add quality tasks without stopping to think about quality. This is why planning is a holistic process.

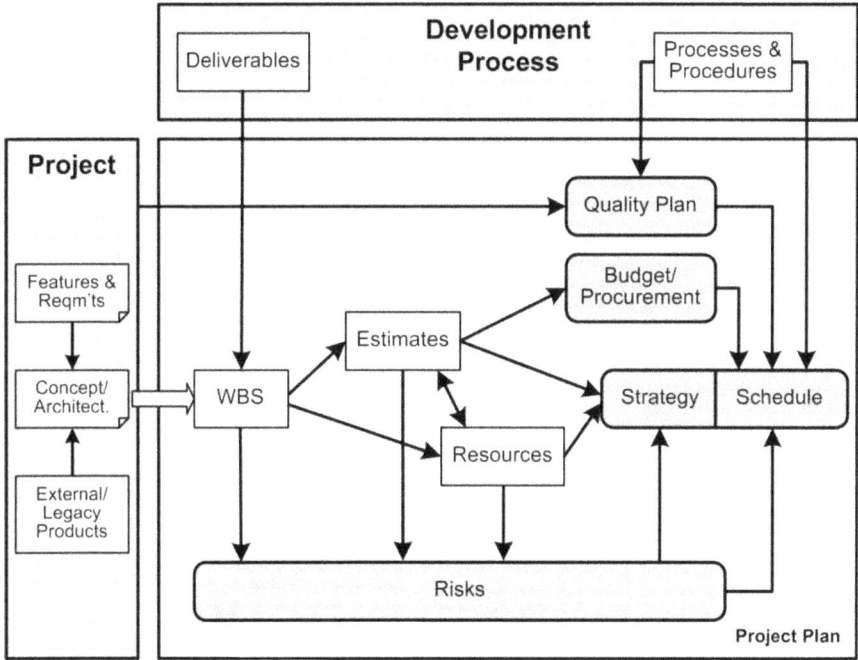

Figure 8.5. The complete planning process for you final iterations.

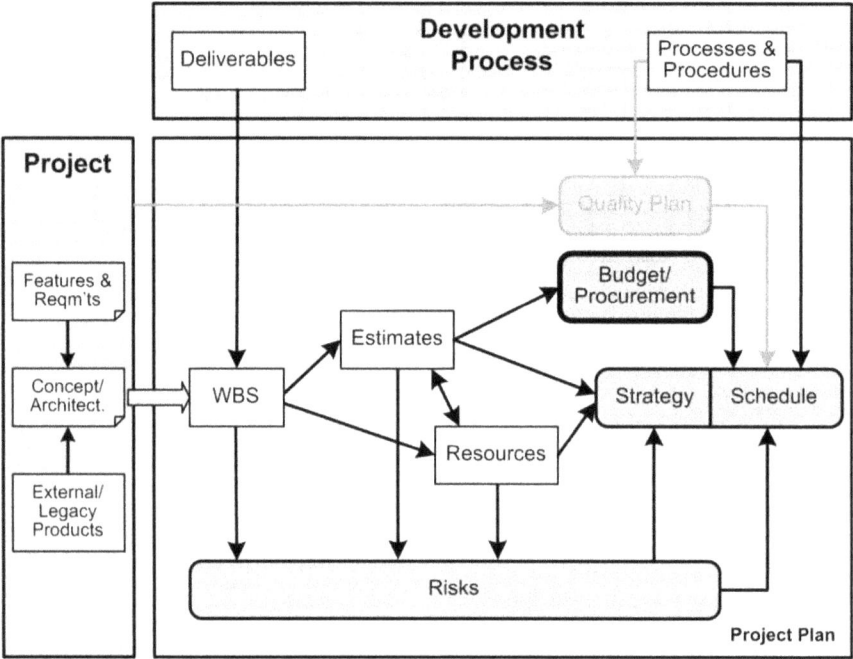

Development Process

Deliverables

Processes & Procedures

Project

Features & Reqm'ts

Concept/ Architect.

External/ Legacy Products

Quality Plan

Budget/ Procurement

Estimates

WBS

Resources

Strategy

Schedule

Risks

Project Plan

9 Spending: Budget and Procurement

Budgets are very important in some organizations. Like your schedule, the budget is based on the WBS. Cost estimates are made when making duration estimates, and follow the same rules. So, we've already addressed some of the key aspects of budgeting.

Costs

Project costs are important since they drive the project business case. Total costs are compared with anticipated revenue to calculate the net business benefits of the project. Usually, these are summarized by a parameter such as return on investment (ROI). The business case may be used to determine if the project is worth doing, to help decide whether to omit a problematic feature, or to compare multiple projects to select which ones to do. Good decisions require reasonable estimates.

Costs you may have to consider include:

- Resources
- Procurement
- Travel
- Training

For most projects, the primary cost is for resources. This is easy to calculate once you have schedule estimates: add some contingency to the planned duration for each resource, and multiply the total hours times the hourly rate. Typically the hourly rate is for a level, for example a senior engineer, rather than for specific resource.

Procurement may include hardware, software or services. Like duration estimates, cost estimates should be made by the owner responsible for the deliverable. Many can be looked up in a catalog or on the internet. A major purchase might require a formal quote, such as for government contracts or for all purchases over a certain dollar amount. Then you should talk with other project managers and with the purchasing department to understand the proper procedures.

Quotes require documentation, so they're difficult to obtain during early planning. Like top-down work estimates you will rely on estimates from experts – people who have done similar things in the past. For a large mechanical frame they will compare size and complexity with some prior structures and use historical cost data to come up with a rough estimate. Fortunately, most organizations can readily access past purchase orders along with applicable specifications. When you look at these, see if there is a history of changes and added costs. If changes are common, you will need some contingency to cover your assessments.

Another thing you might have to budget for is travel. You or team members may have to travel to see customers or deal with suppliers. If you have to fly, can the reservations be made in advance or will they be made just before the trip? There's a big difference in airfare. And don't forget hotels, meals and rental cars. Like costs, you can usually find prior expense reports to gather reasonable estimates. Just make sure you properly estimate the total number of trips. You might even have to put in for a couple of unplanned trips. If you have to travel, there will likely be unplanned trips.

Finally there's training. Typically a project budget only covers training required for that project. You may have to train a team member when they're missing critical expertise. When purchasing complex hardware or software, they may need vendor or third party training. Vendor training is frequently free, for one or two people, but third party training might cost a nominal amount. When you can only send a few people to training, they may have to train the others when they return. This total time for training must be reflected in the schedule. It will add to the duration, and push up the costs of the resources involved. And, unless the training is local, a major cost might be the travel expenses.

If you have to do a detailed cost analysis, your best source of information is the other project managers in your organization. Organizations vary widely in their reporting requirements.

Procurement Process

Many projects don't have a lot of purchased items, so it's not necessary for the project manager to put together a procurement plan. However, when procured items are central to project success, procurement planning is essential to assure those items are available when needed.

Procurement related deliverables and tasks you may have to include in your schedule include:

- Product Specification
- Requesting and Evaluating Quotes
- Getting Approval
- Purchase Order Creation
- Fabrication and Delivery Time
- Setup Time

Small purchases may only require product part numbers. However, something complex like a mechanical fabrication or a printed circuit board will require a set of drawings or a specification describing exactly what you want. A detailed specification can take quite a bit of time for creation and review. Generally you want this work to begin as early as possible.

If quotes are required they will also add time to the process. However, sometimes quotes can be obtained when the specification is almost complete and not approved. This has some risk, but it can shorten the process. When all quotes are in they will be evaluated to select a supplier.

Once you have the specification you may need an approval before you can release a formal purchase order. Both the approval and the purchase order can take time, which should not be overlooked. New project managers tend to ignore the delays these can add, so they don't leave enough time in their schedule. If you have any purchases for your project, you should talk with other project managers, and with the purchasing department, to find out what the ground rules are. Things go smoother and there is less frustration when you follow the rules. Also, if you follow the rules most of the time, when it does becomes necessary to go around the rules, then the people in the procurement chain are more willing to help you.

If the procured item must be fabricated, this adds additional time. Fabrication time may also include a lead time before your vendor can get to your particular order. And if the vendor is not local, there is delivery. If you need it right away, pay the additional cost for overnight delivery. It's cheap compared to people's time. I've seen projects stalled waiting for badly needed equipment that is slowly crossing the country on a truck.

When the procured item is finally received can it be used right out of the box or will there be some time to set it up and learn how to use it? Be realistic and add the appropriate amount of time to the schedule.

When you have a complex part to fabricate, e.g. a printed circuit board, you will also have material or components to procure. These insert another procurement cycle within the procurement cycle of your major part. When you're putting together your schedule you have to make sure that these components are available when needed (see Figure 9.1). Thus you have to figure out when you need to specify the parts and when you have to place their orders. Understanding and managing all of the lead times to make sure that all of this comes together in a timely manner can be a major part of both scheduling and managing the project.

For procurement you not only have to estimate how much money will be spent, but also when it will be committed. Your finance department, for example, might require an approved quarterly spending plan before you can spend any money. By including all procurement in your schedule you have the information they need.

Procurement Risks

Procured parts and procurement activities are another source of risk. Some you might have to consider include:

Functionality: Is it what you really need? Will it do the job that you expect? An engineer might find something close to what is needed and assume he can make it work without too much effort. This is a risk because it may not do what you need. When you're in a situation like this, it's important to recognize it and put time in the schedule to verify that the hardware or software will work. You don't want to hear near the end of the project: "Well, I thought it should work."

Also, fabricated items that don't meet specification or don't work properly may have to be returned for rework. This can be a major schedule risk.

Reliability in your environment: Similarly, issues can arise when the product's specification is marginal for what you need. When hardware or

Purchased Item
Specification
Quotes
Approval
Purchase Order
Fabrication
Delivery
Material/Components
Specification
Approval
Purchase Order
Fabrication
Delivery

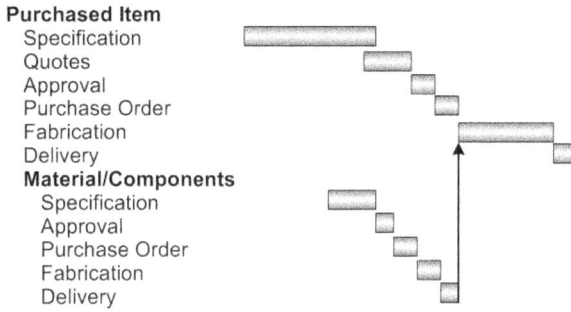

Figure 9.1. A complex procurement process.

software is marginal, this can cause intermittent problems, and some features might not behave as designed. Not only will your product not meet its requirements, but problems associated with marginal behavior can be very difficult to track down and time-consuming to fix.

Delivery time: Identify tasks that cannot start until the product is delivered. You don't want these resources to be held up, especially if they're on the critical path. Ask yourself and the people closest to the purchase: Are all of the lead times reasonable? Does the selected supplier deliver on-time? Your upfront work can prevent some unpleasant surprises.

Vendors: When dealing with vendors go to procurement or other project managers and check out their history. Find out: What is the reputation of the supplier or manufacturer? What is the quality of their products? Again, you want to prevent surprises.

Software updates: Many products have embedded third-party software. That software is constantly being updated – adding new features and improving performance. When you have to update the current version you're using, there are potential issues with backward compatibility, especially when you're skipping over a number of revisions. Changes made to improve the third party software might not be compatible with the way you are using it. Much additional effort will be required to identify the areas of conflict and to rectify the problems.

Many procurement risks are unique to an organization, so you should determine what tends to be unpredictable when major purchases are made.

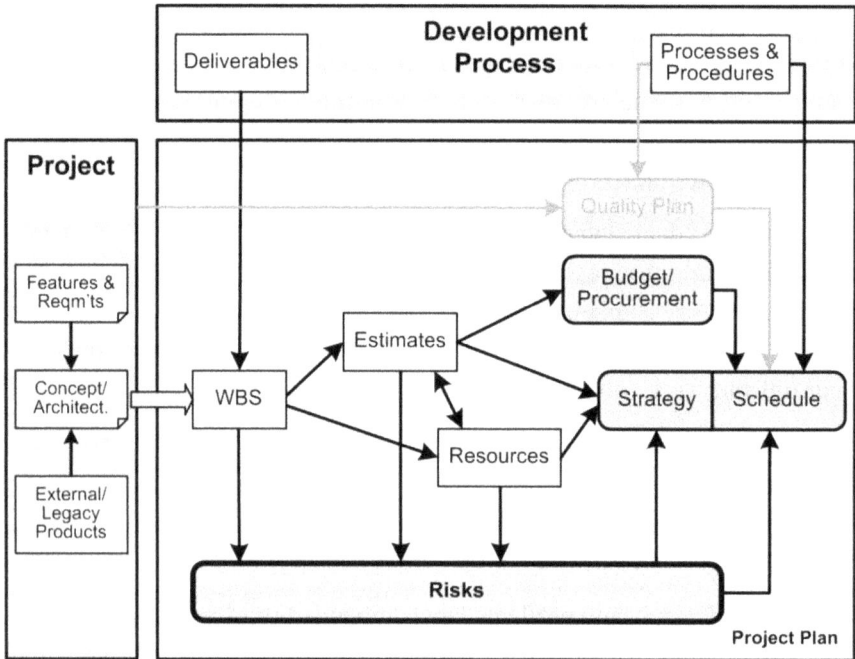

10 A Few More Things About Risk

Schedule Centered Planning requires concurrent risk analysis. Risks are identified and analyzed while creating the WBS, gathering estimates, assigning resources, making major purchases, etc. So there has been quite a bit of discussion about risk in prior chapters. In this chapter we'll look at a few things that are unique to risk. To begin, a good definition of risk is by Dr. David Hillson, the Risk Doctor:

> Risk is uncertainty that matters.

Try to focus on the important risks, those that can push out your end date, cost more money, or significantly impact the deliverables. Don't get bogged down micromanaging things that will ultimately take care of themselves. Make sure you understand what is important and what is not.

Analyzing the Risks

We've seen that a good technique for identifying risks is to listen. As you're working with your project team, listen for where they seem uncertain or doubtful; where requirements are questionable or unclear. Phrases like: "I think . . ." or "We shouldn't have to . . ." signal undue optimism or uncertainty. Then start asking questions to better understand and also quantify what might be a potential problem.

In many organizations the schedule is the most important aspect of the triple constraint. Here it's best to quantify risks in terms of impact to the schedule. Estimate how many days, weeks, or months could be added to a deliverable or to the overall schedule. Don't just use a numerical scale, such as 1 through 5, since this does not convey the true impact of the risk. Knowing a risk can cause a 3 month slip is much more useful than knowing it has a risk value of 5.

Where budgets are tight, cost has priority over schedule. In this situation, try to assess the risks in terms of cost risks, i.e. dollars. Even when the uncertainty is in the duration estimate, you can convert this to cost by considering the number of resources and their hourly rate.

Scope risks are important requirements that you might not be able to meet. These are harder to quantify, as they can apply to diverse requirements. However, they can usually be translated into equivalent schedule or cost risks. For example, you might not meet all performance requirements for a particular deliverable. If so, you will iterate on the development until the deliverable satisfies its performance requirements. Here you can consider a worse case for how long it will take to improve the performance by walking through some scenarios as we did with the three point estimates.

Some scope risks you might have to flag as go/no go – there is a possibility that you just can't meet it. It might be driven by a constraint, such as hardware that you must use, or a fixed delivery date. Whatever the cause, it's important to address it in the strategy or schedule as early as possible.

Record the Risks

Risks should be recorded in a risk log. Then, as the list grows, you can organize it to give you better insight into the project. A risk log is easy to maintain in an Excel spreadsheet. At a minimum, each risk should have:

- *ID*: a unique identification number
- *Description*: Brief description of the risk.
- *Type*: Schedule, cost or scope
- *Deliverable*: Deliverable associated with the risk (might include test, integration, etc.)
- *Probability of Occurrence*: e.g. 25% (low), 50% (medium) and 75% (high)
- *Impact*: Specified in time or cost
- *Score*: Product of the Probability times the Impact
- *Owner*: generally the owner of the associated deliverable
- *Timeframe*: when is the risk likely to occur
- *Resolution*: brief description of how to deal with risk

Associating each risk with a *deliverable* allows you to see which deliverables have the highest risk. When you identify the risks while creating the WBS, assigning owners or generating estimates, then you know the associated WBS deliverable. And, since the deliverables map directly to your schedule, you can add risk information to the schedule and manage risk as you're managing the schedule.

The *score* determines the seriousness of a risk. A higher score means a more serious risk. If all of your risks are schedule or all are cost, then you can sort on the score. If not, you have to use the *type* to sort the schedule and cost risks separately. As project manager, you should continuously monitor those with the highest scores.

The *owner* is responsible for dealing with the risk. Knowing the *timeframe*, you should periodically contact the owners to determine status of upcoming risks. Also, you can sort on owner to see if any one owner has to deal with too much risk.

When a risk has a high probability of occurring, it will have a low probability of not occurring. If you have a major risk with a high probability of occurring, you should assume it will occur and then determine what you can do to mitigate the effect. For example, don't say a deliverable will take three months with a high likelihood it will take four. Rather, say: It will take four months, and then explore what is necessary to pull it into three. When you assume it will occur you see things from a different perspective and your thinking changes. If you leave three months in the schedule, you will likely just hope it doesn't take four. When you put four months in the schedule you may be forced to be creative.

Deal with Risks

It's not enough to identify your risks you have to deal with them. There are different ways you can deal with a specific risk:

- Accept
- Avoid
- Transfer
- Mitigate

You can *accept* that a risk may occur and deal with the consequence if it does. Usually these are risks where the probability and impact are both low.

Sometimes you can *avoid* or eliminate that which can cause the risk. For example, you might eliminate a problematic requirement, acquire a subject matter expert, ease up on a tight performance spec, or delay a specific feature until a later release. With inadequate resources you can negotiate with management for what you need. Many risks exist simply because of optimistic assumptions. Using range estimates and walking through scenarios to eliminate undue optimism will also reduce or eliminate those risks.

You might be able to *transfer* ownership of the risk to a third party, outside of your project. Buying insurance is the classic way of transferring ownership, but most project risks are not readily covered by insurance. Hiring consultants or other experts to do the work is another possibility. You will need assurance that they have the capabilities, and you might want to back that up with a penalty clause in their contract.

For many of the major risks, you are expected to be proactive and take action within your project plan to *mitigate* the risk – that is, reduce the likelihood that the risk will occur, or the impact if it does occur. This is best done when creating the strategy. When looking at the DAS strategy we discussed how you might deal with a late resource, a complex deliverable and performance issues. Adding contingency, such as a buffer, at the end of the schedule is another way to mitigate risk.

With a little imagination and an understanding of what's important, you have more leeway than you might think. As you manage more projects and get used to thinking strategically, you will just automatically deal with the major risks as you identify them.

Brainstorming

You will identify many risks during the early stages of planning, e.g., while creating the WBS, assigning resources and estimating work. As the plan is solidifying, and most of the resources have been assigned, then it can be useful to have a brainstorming session. Not only is this another technique to identify risks, it is also a good exercise in team building. The team walks through the project together, gets to see the potential problems, and can start developing solutions for those problems.

Brainstorming involves your entire team and, if possible, some outside experts. Gather them into a room, post the WBS and the strategy on a wall, and have the participants take some time to review and ask questions about both. Ask them to think about the challenges they anticipate and what they might be unclear about. Once they understand the big picture, you can begin the brainstorming session.

Two simple rules to remember are:

1. *Write down everything without discussion* – throw nothing out. A ridiculous statement might trigger somebody else to think about a real risk.

2. *Make sure all of the participants are involved* – non-participants might be shy about contributing, so ask each one if he or she has anything to add.

You want team participation, so you should not drive the discussions, merely record what is said. However, if things seem to be stuck, you might have questions ready to restart the discussion.

Brainstorming will produce a lengthy, unstructured list of potential risks. When you're done with the brainstorming you have to process the list before it is useful. Because you do not throw anything out (Rule 1) you will have a lot of garbage and some items that are not really risks. Also, since the risks were just thrown out randomly, the list is not organized.

Resist the temptation to just put the list into an Excel spreadsheet, have team members fill in impact and likelihood of occurrence, and then sort on score. If you do this without removing the garbage and non-risks, useful information can become buried in the garbage and non-risks.

Before ending the brainstorming session, review the list to eliminate the obvious garbage and those items that are not really risks. If an item is meaningless and nobody can convert it to a real risk the eliminate it. If an item has a 100% change of occurring, such as: "We have no test plan", then it is not a risk, there is no uncertainty. However, since it was raised to identify a potential concern, identify what that concern was. For example, not having a test plan could mean that testing is not understood, that it could be very complex, or that it might take longer than planned. If the latter, you might replace it with: "Testing might take longer than planned." Then the project manager can work with those responsible for the test plan to determine as quickly as possible how much time will be required.

With the list trimmed, associate a deliverable with each element and sort on the deliverables. Here you can see if you can consolidate two or more similar risks. After you've made appropriate consolidations, move the risks to the risk log you started earlier, and fill in impact, likelihood and owner.

Example from a Real Brainstorming Session

The following is part of a risk log from an actual brainstorming session. It is for a complex computerized electro-mechanical system, and because of unmanaged risks, the project was significantly late and an important window of opportunity was missed. This cost the company millions of dollars and resulted in a number of people losing their jobs.

For this project, this brainstorming session was the only way of identifying risk. Over 50 risks were identified and immediately put into a spreadsheet. The group then added Probability and Impact assessments, along with a proposed Response of how to deal with each risk. Each description and response was rather lengthy, so that when printed out, the log was three pages of very fine print – barely readable, and mostly ignored!

Table 10.1 lists the top 10 risks cleaned up to make the descriptions shorter and generic. Probability and Impact were each assessed on scale of 1 to 5. Also, three of the risks are not really risks:

2	Test plan/strategy is not yet complete
8	Hardware specification not finalized
18	Potential for lots of change requests

The first two are statements of the status of the project at the time the brainstorming session was held. In fact, neither was a problem for the project. The third is true for just about any project, and changes must be properly managed when they are proposed. For a project like this with a firm deadline, changes should only be accepted after very detailed analysis, and only if adequate resources are included with the change request.

Below the top 10 list, Table 10.2 shows those risks associated with Application Specific Integrated Circuits (ASICs). The ASICs were one of the major reasons for not meeting the schedule. However, only one ASIC risk (# 4) is in the top 10 list, and it is near the bottom of the list. Note also that for the ASICs most of the risks have a probability of 1 or 2. The optimistic engineers who made the assessments did not feel any of these was likely to occur. While this might be valid for any one of them, there are quite a few and the probability of something going wrong is very high. Because of the low scores, they were down at the bottom of the list, and they were just accepted with no attempt to avoid or mitigate. They should

ID	Risk - Description	Prob	Impact	Score
2	Test plan/strategy is not yet complete	5	5	25
5	Test suites might not provide 100% coverage	4	5	20
18	Potential for lots of change requests	4	5	20
35	Driver testing may require multiple test cycles	4	5	20
16	High power and heat may impact reliability if not enough cooling	3	5	15
30	Development and integration delays due to unknown technical problems	3	5	15
34	Currently don't have capability to test all scenarios	3	4	12
4	Delays in the Signal Processing ASIC delivery	2	5	10
8	Hardware specification not finalized	2	5	10
13	Cosmetic design may impact delivery date	2	5	10

Table 10.1. An example of top 10 risks.

ID	Risk - Description	Prob	Impact	Score
4	Delays in the Signal Processing ASIC delivery	2	5	10
7	Delays in the Parametric ASIC delivery	2	4	8
12	Signal Processing features might not fit in ASIC	4	2	8
19	Development resource conflicts at ASIC Developers	1	5	5
24	Signal Processing ASIC does not fully implement key new functionality	1	5	5
25	The updated interface in the Parametric ASIC does not work correctly	1	5	5
32	Signal Processing ASIC has problems with synchronous pattern generation	1	5	5
31	Major revision required for firmware in Signal Proc ASIC	1	4	4
23	ASICs might not fully support legacy functionality	1	3	3

Table 10.2. Those risks associated with ASICs.

have been combined into a couple of risks with high probability and high impact. Then an assessment of the magnitude could be made, such as by looking at worst case scenarios. With the impact identifying the potential slip, then management should have been informed of a serious problem.

So it's really important to go through and clean up everything on any brainstorming lists. The shorter and more organized your risk log is, the more useful and more manageable it will be.

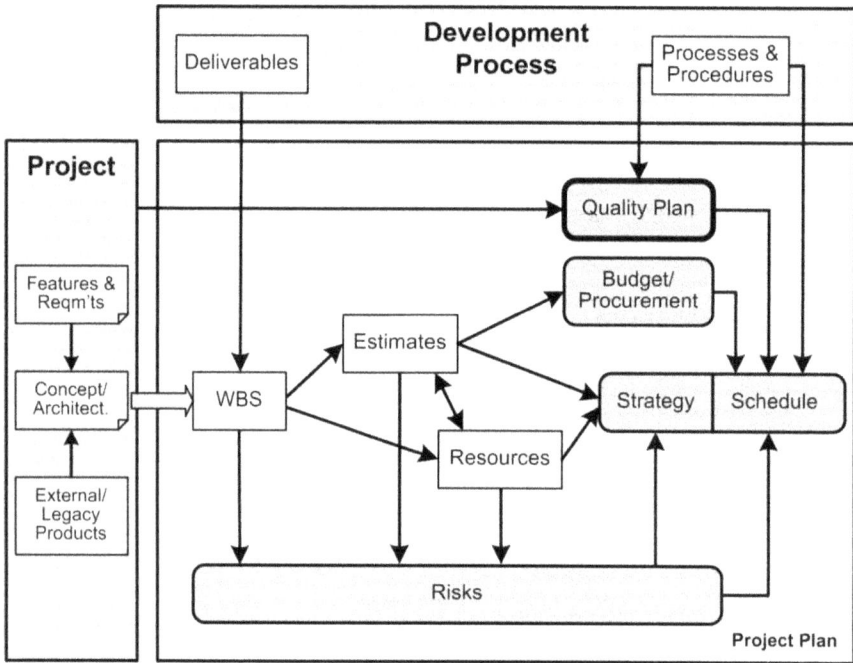

11 Do It Right: Quality

Many projects fail not because they miss the schedule or are over budget but because the quality of the end product is just not acceptable. So let's see what quality is and then see what a project manager must do to make sure that the project produces a quality result.

A fairly common definition of quality comes from Philip Crosby:

Quality is conformance to requirements.

It is certainly well known by project managers. It's a few words, catchy, and easy to remember. However, if you asked what conformance to requirements really means, you would probably get some hesitation. Most would expect it to be self-explanatory, in which case, they don't really understand it.

The key word in this definition is Requirements. Crosby means a lot more than just a specification or a feature list describing the end product. Rather, he is talking about all of the requirements that assure all involved in the project get what they need. Therefore, because the word requirements, as Crosby uses it, is not generally understood, I would substitute "user's needs" for a working definition of Quality:

Quality is conformance to user's needs.

It is brief and has two key words, users and needs, that we need to explore.

Aspects of Quality

There are three aspects that have to be addressed when considering quality:

1. *Acceptance criteria* – When addressing the user's needs, it is important to understand what's acceptable. You need to do at least that much. But, if it will cost you time and resources, you do not want to do much more than what is acceptable.

2. *Quality assurance (QA)* – This is doing the right things to make sure that quality is built in. Frequently this is defined by your organization's processes. In addition, there are challenges to quality that the project manager can address to assure good quality.

3. *Quality control (QC)* – Someone must verify that all deliverables meet quality standards – that they are acceptable to their users. Testing is a major form of quality control.

Quality Measures – Acceptance Criteria

There will be many ways to measure the acceptability or quality of your delivered product. Most will be unique to your product and will be derived from the products requirements. For most requirements the acceptance criteria will be obvious. For example, a physical parameter such as maximum weight. Others will require some interpretation such as the need to operate for five years in a remote environment. Special tests to simulate five years of life will have to be agreed to.

Common acceptance criteria that are specific to quality include:

Reliability: At its simplest, we can define reliability as operating without any errors. But, for many complex projects, this can be too restrictive. So when we talk about reliability, we really mean operating free of major errors. Your organization should define criteria for establishing what is a major error and what is not desirable but could be permitted.

Performance: Generally related to speed of operation, it could also refer to accuracy, and even size. You may have to respond to a user query within 1 second, or process a real time data input within 10 milliseconds. For your automobile, you may have to get better than 40 miles per gallon of gas.

Robustness: How to respond to error conditions. Does a computer just crash? Is that acceptable? Do you just notify the user that there is a problem or do you do everything possible to recover? Like the others, robustness can be quite complex to define exactly what it means.

Usability: You could have wonderful features, but if your customers have great difficulty using your product, they will go to a competitor that does not have all the features, but is easier to use. In my experience you need somebody close to the end users to specify and evaluate usability. For many products, developers really don't understand the end user. This is especially true for software that is intended for non-software professionals.

Testability: Are those responsible for test able to test the final product? Can they create all of the necessary inputs and scenarios to replicate actual usage? Can they make measurements to verify that a test is successful or not, where success also that there are no unwanted side effects.

These are just a few of the many ways we describe quality in terms of the user experience. You must look at your products and your projects to identify what are most important to your users.

Challenges to Quality

A project Manager does not have to be an expert in quality to assure a quality product. There are many challenges that are part of managing a project and successfully managing these will improve the quality of the work to develop the end product. These include:

Poor requirements: Requirements may be ambiguous, incomplete, or simply not doable.

Poor development practices: Shortcuts are taken during development, typically to meet tight schedules. This directly impacts quality.

Inadequate testing: Tests are developed without sufficient information or tight schedules limit the time for testing.

Us vs. Them: on multi-disciplinary projects, one group – Us – sees all problems as caused by another group – Them. Basically these groups do not work together as a team. Common ones are Development vs. QA, or Manufacturing vs. Development.

Unrealistic deadlines: Individuals or even entire teams are forced to take shortcuts that compromise their work. This can be the cause of, or make worse the Us vs. Them problem.

Poor communications: Necessary information is not shared between individuals and groups.

Focus on fun: Some individuals would rather focus on the fun aspects of the projects and gloss over what they consider drudgery, which can be very important to others on the project.

Product complexity: Complex products frequently have difficulty meeting all of the quality requirements. However, organizations that develop complex products also have processes in place to deal with complexity.

Chain of Quality

Looking at a simple example highlights what I like to call the chain of quality. It shows how quality flows through your development process, pointing out the users and their needs. A simple, fairly common process flow is shown in Figure 11.1. The flow is not meant to imply a waterfall. Thus the Requirements do not have to be complete before the Architecture can start. But the top level requirements have to be known and understood before meaningful architectural work can begin.

To identify users and their needs consider the Interface Design Document. It is used by the creators of the

- Detailed Design
- End Product
- Test Procedures
- User Documents

Therefore it must meet the needs of all of these users. Frequently the designers and developers will work together and have an intimate knowledge of the product. For them, omissions in the Interface Design are easily filled in from their working knowledge. However, this might not be the case for those creating comprehensive tests or user documentation. I've seen developers have to stop what they are doing, get on an airplane and travel half way around the world to fix a customer problem caused by inadequate user documentation. The users don't have the detailed knowledge that the developers have, so they cannot see the need to do things that are not explicitly defined in their documentation.

The architecture is another good example because it is used by Development, Test and Documentation, and it also drives your WBS, the foundation for your entire project plan. In both cases, to meet the user's needs the documents must be complete, unambiguous and verifiable. In fact, this applies to all the documents.

It's clear from the process flow that all documents are needed by a diverse set of users. Those users, or a designated representative, should be part the document reviews. No document should be released until the applicable users verify that it will meet their needs.

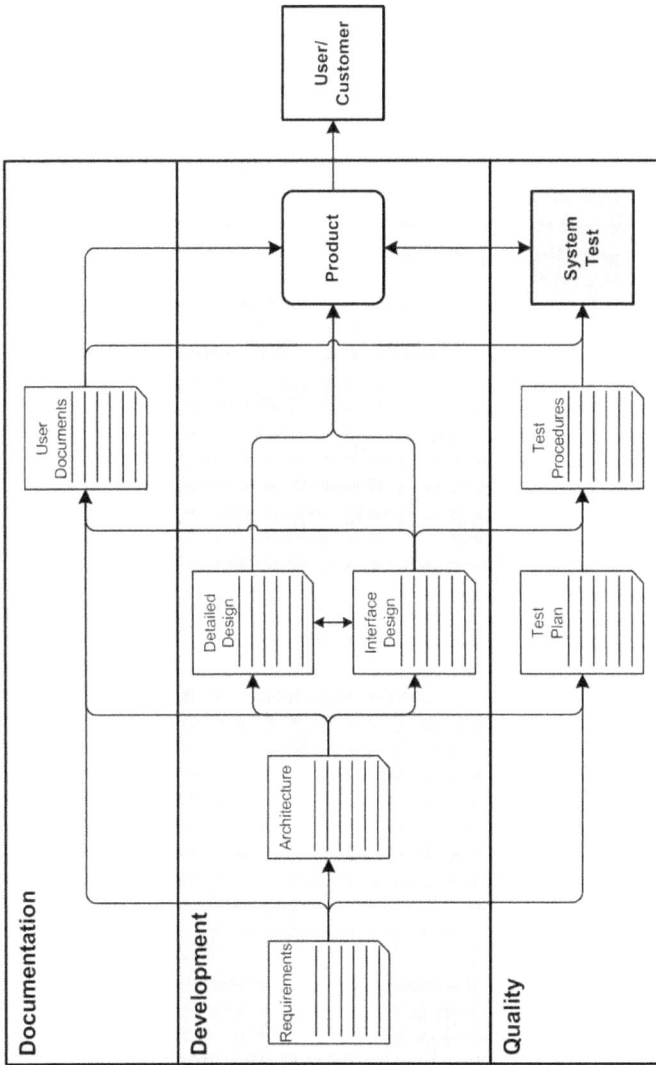

Figure 11.1. A simple process flow to highlight the chain of quality.

Standards and Procedures

Quality assurance usually lays out a number of standards and procedures to be followed when developing a specific product.

Standards

Standards are the rules and guidelines that tell us how to do things. One common form of standard is a document template. Templates define what information must be included in each document and how it is to be arranged. They make it easier to generate the documents and assure uniformity. The developer does not have to start from scratch, and is less likely to omit important information. Templates work best when accompanied by completed documents, that clarify what is required and may contain much information can be reused.

If your organization does not provide the needed templates, look on the web. However, before using them, work with senior people to make sure they are appropriate, and to identify any customization required.

One problem with documentation is that many people are not good at it. Poor writing skills can cause ambiguity, omissions and possibly even errors, and can add unnecessary time to the development of the document. Thus all documents should be kept as simple as possible, with no more information than is needed. One way to do this is to use tables and lists as much as possible. They are concise and much easier to create.

Consider an example of physical device characteristics for a consumer-oriented electronic device shown on the next page. A couple of sections from a formal document are translated into an equivalent table. The table is more concise and is a lot easier to fill in. Thus it is easier to use, saves time and reduces errors. This can be especially important when you have resources writing in a language that is not their native language.

Templates are just one type of standard. You might also have design, interface and development standards. For example, software standards address module size, naming conventions and coding standards; hardware standards address design for test and design for manufacturability to guarantee that the final product can be manufactured economically.

You have to assess what standards are appropriate for your projects. If they

4.3. Device Physical Characteristics

4.3.1   Powering:

The device shall be powered by an external transformer. The transformer shall be included in the packaging for the device.

4.3.2   Power Failure Performance:

Power disruptions of 250 ms or less shall be handled without severe consequences.

In the event of a power failure, information stored in volatile memory (i.e. RAM) shall be retained for a minimum of 24 hours.

4.3.3   Battery Life

Each unit shall have battery for backup power in the event of a power failure. The customer shall not have to replace batteries more often than once each year under normal operating conditions.

In the event that the battery power is low, a "Low Battery" indication shall be displayed on the screen.

Figure 11.2. Typical requirements for a consumer electronics device.

4.3. Physical Device Characteristics		
4.3.1	Powering	An external transformer shall be supplied.
4.3.2	Power Failure Performance	Handle power disruptions of 250 ms or less without severe consequences. Volatile memory shall be retained for at least 24 hours during a power failure.
4.3.3	Battery Life	Batteries to last more than one year under normal operating conditions. "Low Battery" indication on the screen.

Figure 11.3. Requirements presented in tabular form.

don't exist, define the bare minimum you can do for significant payback. For example, while a checklist is useful for a code walkthrough, doing walkthrough without a checklist is far better than not doing them. Over time the checklist will evolve. Make sure to add the appropriate tasks to the schedule since the work will take time. Then identify the tasks before they are due to let people know that they have to do the work.

Policies and Procedures

Policies and procedures also tell people how to perform specific activities such as making a major purchase, performing a design review or doing a code walkthrough. One important quality control procedure is the design review. All internal deliverables should be reviewed to make sure they are acceptable. Each document in the sample process flow should have a design review prior to release. Since design reviews are very important and apply to a wide range of projects, they will be discussed in more detail in the next section.

Inspections are another important procedure. The customer or a regulatory agency might want to come in to inspect your product. Or, you might have an internal group that inspects things to assure that everybody does things in a consistent way. With software you have code walkthroughs, where peers review the code to look for errors and to make sure that it follows the published standards. I've seen more than a few subtle bugs uncovered in a walkthrough that might have taken a long time to find with testing.

For hardware there are many types of analysis that must be performed. Mechanical systems require structural and thermal analysis. State-of-the-art printed circuit boards also require a thermal analysis and an extensive timing analysis.

The list goes on, and again you need to look at your particular organization to see what kind of quality control procedures they have in place. Ultimately however, quality depends on your project team: Are they working together as a team and do they have the knowledge and understanding of the quality processes? In some organizations quality is part of the culture and everybody understands the quality processes. However, in others individuals know very little about quality. This is something you will have to assess at the organization where you work.

Reviews

Many processes require a number of documents and each must be reviewed prior to release. This review is to assure that the document and anything produced from the document will meet the needs of all of its users. That's why reviews are critical to quality.

First, the project manager needs to identify all reviews that will be performed, and add each to the schedule. Typically reviews will take a day or two, but a complex review can extend to a week or more. There will also be an update following the review to resolve the issues the review is sure to uncover.

Key users and domain experts who have not been involved in the development activities should make up the review team. The users make sure it meets their needs, and the domain experts provide an unbiased assessment of the overall content. Together, these must cover all aspects of the document under review. It can be a major problem when, for example, there is no one who understands a major interface, other than the designer.

During the review it is important to check for both correctness and completeness. I have found that most people do reasonably well when they check for correctness, at least within their domain of knowledge. People are more than happy to point out what they think might be wrong. So this aspect generally gets good coverage in reviews.

However, it's more important to review for completeness, and this is an area where many reviews fall short. Technical people will dive right in and look at the details to see if they are correct or not. But they're really not that good at standing back, looking at a document in its totality, and assessing what might be missing. As a project manager you must be proactive. Assure yourself that when people are reviewing documents, they are looking for omissions as well as correctness.

In a review, all opinions count. Although they will all have equal weight, the opinions of the junior people and non-specialists must be heard and evaluated. This is another area where you might have to deal with an us vs. them problem. Senior developers might want to ignore comments from quality, operations or marketing. In this case, it's important for you to establish a dialogue. Sometimes a reviewer has a valid concern but is not able to express it in terms the developer understands. Patient, emphatic questions will help identify the real issue so that everybody understands it. Then you can assess its importance.

During the review, somebody should be assigned to take minutes. At the end of the review walk through what has and has not been agreed to. The minutes should also include action items. Each action item should identify who is responsible, along with a date for when it should be resolved. When individuals have too many other things to do, they tend to ignore these things. Then, it is your responsibility to track them and make sure that all issues are resolved in a timely manner.

Finally, make sure that the document being reviewed is baselined. It's important that everybody working on the project is using the same documents. A different version is a different document. So, once approved, a document cannot be changed without going through a formal process, which must include another review. This should be addressed in your organization's configuration management and change control processes. These are also important aspects of quality which the project manager must understand and enforce across the project.

Testing

Your developed product must undergo rigorous testing to make sure that it meets all of its acceptance criteria. For most projects, this is the primary focus of Quality Control.

Those who do the testing are often overlooked in the chain of quality. One reason is that frequently Development vs. Test is a typical us vs. them situation. When testing does not uncover the major faults in a product, it is easy to say that the problem is poor testing, or lack of testing skills. However, often, the root cause is that the development documents do not meet the needs of Quality. The best way to deal with this is to bring these groups together as early as possible. Have one or more meetings to discuss requirements and what they mean. These should be informal question and answer sessions that bring those responsible for test up to speed and foster teamwork between the groups.

Testing starts with the test plan. It identifies and outlines all of the tests that will be performed. If a test is not in the test plan, it will not be performed. So it needs to be complete.

The primary document driving the test plan is the requirements. If the requirements are not complete, if they are ambiguous, or if they are not verifiable, then the test plan will be missing tests or specifying tests that are not appropriate. For this reason it's good to create the test plan as early as possible and have it reviewed by the developers. This gets development and QA working together early, and if there are differences in the way each interprets the requirements, these will be identified early. Given the different perspectives of the two groups, it is not uncommon to have ambiguities interpreted differently.

The test plan drives the test procedures. As the process flow shows, developing the procedures may require other input from the developers such as an interface document. Again, it's important that the interface document meet the needs of the testers. This is why working together, or what is referred to as concurrent engineering, is so important. Establishing a close working relationship as the test plan is being developed will carry over to the procedures and to testing itself. Then you have a fully functional team, not separate working groups.

Nonconformance

As you go through these standards, policies and procedures – reviewing documents, walking through the code, testing the end product, etc. – it's inevitable that you will have non-conformance, generally referred to as defects or bugs. While this is not part of planning – nobody plans to have defects – it's important to round out the discussion on quality.

All defects and bugs must be recorded. If you don't write them down, they will be forgotten, and they will be overlooked.

Make sure they are properly categorized. Standard bug tracking systems have about a dozen different fields of information that need to be filled in. For example, there are some to identify where the bug is. What software module or what particular area on a printed circuit board? With more details provided, it's easier to find and resolve the problem.

It's also important to know how serious the problem is. Then you can focus efforts on the most serious problems and ignore those that are just a minor annoyance.

You should keep track of the most serious defects, as well as the trend in total defects. Is the team finding more or fewer defects? Is the defect list growing or shrinking? How serious are the defects they are finding? This is just one way of establishing the health of your project and validating when you might be finished. If you're schedule says you'll be done in a week, but the total number of unfixed defects is increasing, then you're probably not going to meet your schedule. But, a crash effort can work miracles.

Do It Right

A major problem which was listed in the challenges to quality is an unrealistic timeline. A deadline is specified, and the project manager must put together a schedule to meet that deadline. Here the time allocated to development and testing is not driven by estimates of total work.

If the schedule is unrealistic, developers are forced to cut corners. There will also be poor communications among the developers, as individuals need to focus on their own work. However, communications between developers has a lot to do with project success, and it has a lot to do with its quality. It is also essential for teamwork. Teamwork takes time, but it will shorten the development cycle in the long run. Much of the front end work can be made a little bit faster without teamwork but, when the work of the individuals has to be integrated together, the testing and problem resolution will take a lot longer.

If there is still a lot of pressure to finish the project as soon as possible, testing will be inadequate. Defects added during development are not found during testing and your customers become your testers. Then there will be a long maintenance cycle to fix the issues they find. So even though you've shipped, the project continues long past what it would have taken if you had done it right!

Also, since the resources don't free up when planned, the next project starts off late. It will also have resource conflicts as people are moving back and forth between projects. This moving back and forth causes a lot of context switching, reducing the developer's effectiveness, which can also cause errors, which leads to even more maintenance. This leads to what might be called a quality death spiral. It's a vicious cycle: your project suffers because the one before it was late, and the one after yours will suffer a similar fate.

Unfortunately, in many situations there's not a lot you can do about unrealistic deadlines. So what can you do?

First, make sure you focus on the user needs early. Get good requirements and a good architecture.

Then, start testing as soon as possible. Don't wait until near the end of the project to identify and fix defects. As we've seen, early test and integration is a benefit of incremental development, so a good strategy can do a lot to assure that quality is built in.

Also, when you crate your strategy you need to set project priorities. You want to get those things that are most important done as early as possible. This assures that even if you're not finished, you have something that is useful to your end-user.

Early integration also helps deal with another challenge – communications. The developers have to work together both before and during the frequent integration cycles. When integration is done very late and resources are under pressure to develop quickly, they can go a long time and do a lot of work with minimum communications with other project team members.

Having a partially functional product early allows you to start burn in or run in testing. Continuous overnight and weekend testing will identify defects that simple functional tests do not. Frequently, it's a challenge just to run overnight. But, as you get it to run overnight and over weekends, it's a tremendous team motivator to see the product really take shape. And, of course, you're identifying and fixing some of the worst defects.

And, before you're done, you have something usable that you can share with an end user. Give them something they can play with and they will find defects that you cannot. Again, you're increasing quality and getting valuable feedback from a customer.

Grass Roots Efforts to Help Do It Right

If processes are lacking at your organization you should consider grass roots initiatives. I have seen, and been involved in a number of grassroots initiatives that have fixed some of these shortcomings. A lot of them come from senior technical people. Others come from discussions between project managers and the senior technical people. But basically, somebody took the initiative to get them started.

- Instituting formal design reviews
- Creating coding standards
- Performing code walkthroughs.
- Creating document templates
- Establishing a core team of senior people to resolve issues

These major grassroots initiatives were driven or facilitated from the project management level in the organization, not from the top. So there is a lot you can do to improve quality even if you are in a situation where the quality processes are not adequate. You must look at the projects within your organization, determine where the processes are missing, inadequate, or could just use improvement, and then get creative. Just remember to start off small and simple. It will be more acceptable and many times a small change can have a large effect.

You can make a difference.

Appendix

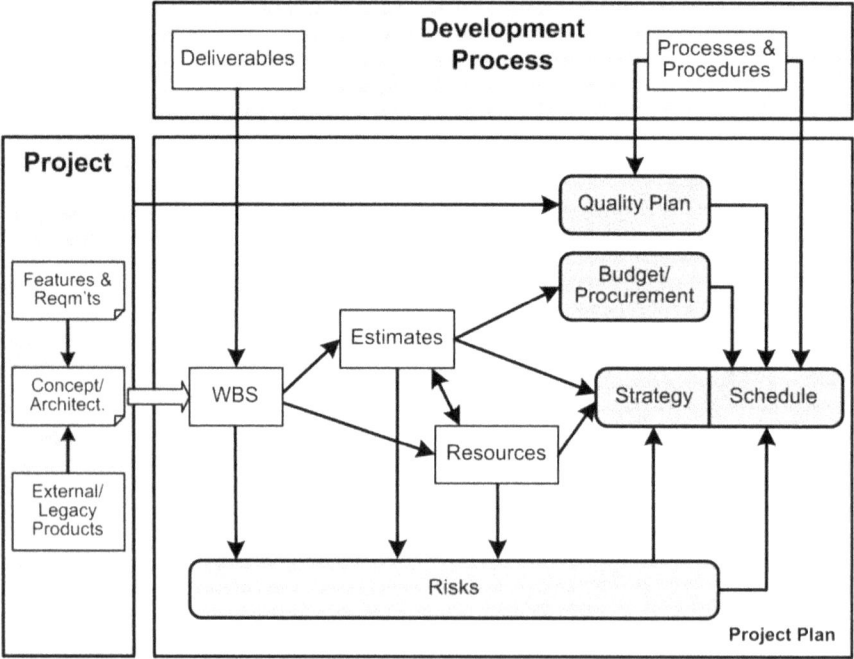

Development Process

Deliverables

Processes & Procedures

Project

Features & Reqm'ts

Concept/ Architect.

External/ Legacy Products

WBS

Estimates

Resources

Quality Plan

Budget/ Procurement

Strategy

Schedule

Risks

Project Plan

Appendix A. Making Microsoft Project Your Planning Tool

A properly created schedule is a project plan. Microsoft Project is a commonly used scheduling tool with features that allow you to turn it into a powerful planning tool. That is, you can create custom Fields, Filters, Groups and Views, which, as we will see, help you manage your entire project, not just the schedule.

There are many good books that you can use to learn about the features of project. So it will be assumed that you either have one of the many reference books or you have a working knowledge of Project. This appendix will show you how to take advantage of the custom features so you can use Project more effectively and make planning easier. Hence it will focus on the dialog boxes you use to customize the Fields, Filters, Groups and Views.

All of the dialogs presented are from Project 2007, but most are identical in Project 2010. Where they differ, the differences are minor, and the information presented here will work in 2010.

The main difference between Project 2007 and 2010 is how to get to the dialogs. Project 2007 has menus, and the user must select a drop down menu, select the appropriate item in the menu, and, where necessary, select an item in a submenu. Project 2010 has tabs. The user selects the proper tab, then the appropriate item on that tab and in many cases selects a sub-item from a drop down menu. In each section the path to bring up the desired dialog will be represented by a table of the following format:

Version	Menu/Tab	Item	Sub-item
2007	Menu	Menu Item	Submenu Item
2010	Tab	Item	Sub-item

Fields

Project calculates and stores everything you want to know about your schedule, and many things you might even be afraid to ask about. Project also provides customizable fields to store information that you feel is important but is not schedule specific. Custom fields can store text, cost, dates, flags, numbers, etc. There is limited ability to do custom calculations and, if appropriate, you can display the contents with graphical symbols, such as red, yellow and green stoplights.

Fields are where you start to customize Project. With appropriate fields in place the filters, groups and views become much more useful. Some of the custom fields I have set up to help me manage large schedules include:

Field	Type	Usage
Owner	Text	Resource responsible for a deliverable or task; generally the assigned resource, but multiple or alternate resources may be assigned; Also, Summary tasks have an owner where they can't have an assigned resource.
Stage	Text	Stage in integration strategy; helps to focus on one stage when developing or managing the schedule.
Quality	Flag	Tasks that are quality activities; helps create and isolate the quality plan within Project.
Risk	Flag	Deliverables or tasks with associated risks; helps create and isolate the risks within Project.
Risks	Text	Risk numbers from the Risk Log; reference back to the risk log if more information needed.
Risk Level	Text	Indictor to assign High, Medium or Low risk level to tasks flagged as risks
Procurement	Flag	Task associated with procurement; helps create and isolate the procurement plan within Project.
Look Ahead Date	Date	A date 2 weeks beyond the current date; helps identify all tasks that are overdue or due within the next two weeks.

| Location | Text | Geographic locations; isolate all tasks for a specific location. |
| Product/Program | Text | Product or Program that tasks are assigned to; useful when many schedules are integrated into a master schedule. |

Each of these can be used to filter or reorganize a large schedule. When I have a schedule with hundreds of tasks, ten or more resources and multiple integration stages, I can focus on a single owner or a single stage. Being able to focus like this makes creation and updating a schedule a lot easier.

Many of these fields apply to both summary and regular tasks. However, I only assign a Stage to those summary tasks representing low level deliverables that are referenced in the integration strategy. I do not assign one to the highest level deliverables – such as DAS or Data Processing – as these have been broken down and their lower level deliverables are integrated across multiple stages. Thus they are not contained within a single stage.

Similarly, having an Owner assigned to a summary task is very useful since it not appropriate to assign resources to summary tasks. However, I do not assign an Owner to a high level deliverable, such as Integration and Test, which has multiple owners for the deliverables below.

I have three flags that I use in most of my schedules: Quality, Risk and Procurement. With the Quality flag I can identify all tasks, such as tests and reviews, that would be considered part of the quality plan, and create a filter to look at only those tasks. Then by running that filter I can see my quality activities and who is responsible for each. I can review the list to make sure it is complete, and, during execution, I can quickly check to see if there are any upcoming quality activities to make sure they are not overlooked. I can do similar things with the Risk and Procurement flags.

While you could benefit from using many of these fields, you should think about your projects, how you might like to group or filter your tasks, and what project information distinguishes those groups. Then you can define your own custom fields.

Creating and Managing Custom Fields

You create new custom fields and modify existing ones through the Custom Fields dialog. The most direct way to access this dialog is:

Version	Menu/Tab	Item	Sub-item
2007	Tools	Customize	Fields . . .
2010	Project	Custom Fields	

You can also right click in a header column and then select Custom Fields. . .

This brings up the Custom Fields Dialog box:

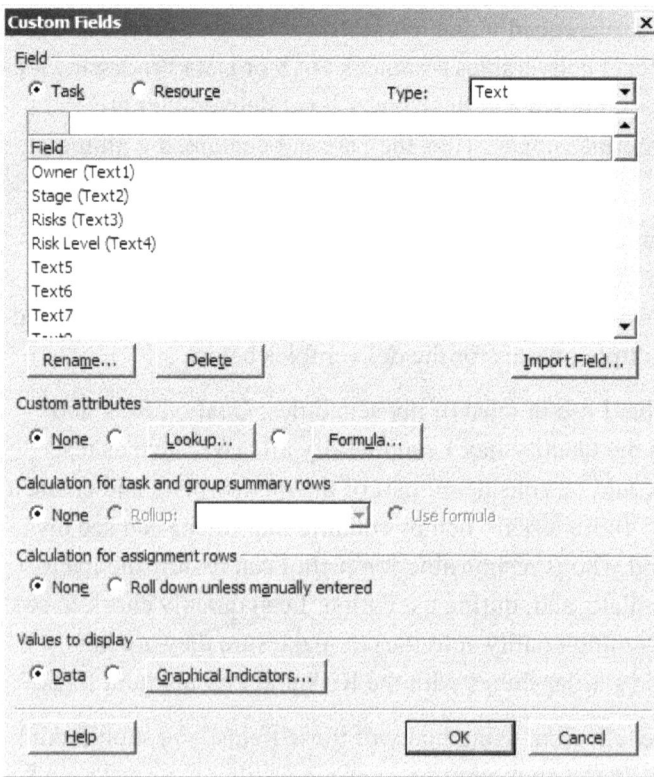

By default it brings up the text fields, and you can see that Text1 through Text4 have been renamed based on fields in the list. When you use a field you should always click on the **Rename . . .** button and give it a unique, meaningful name. The name will show up when you display a column of that data, and it will be obvious when you go to this dialog which fields are in use and which are not.

Lookup Tables

Frequently text fields such as Owner and Stage, will have a few values. These can be placed in a Lookup Table by clicking on the **Lookup . . .** button. On the next page is the Lookup Table for the Stages in the DAS Software schedule. With a lookup table, Project provides a dropdown for the individual entries. This assures consistency which is important when filtering or grouping on these fields.

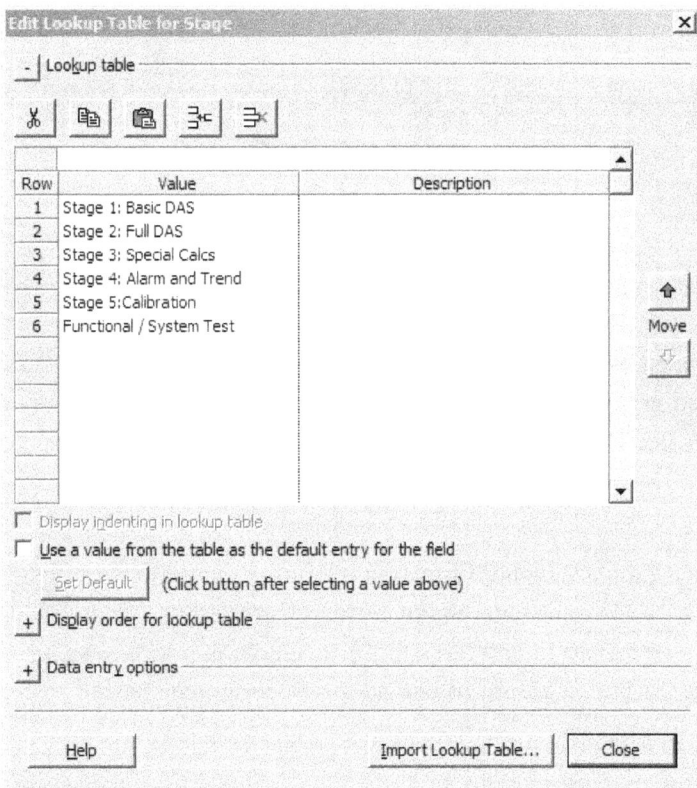

The order that you see in the dialog is the order in which they will appear in the list. If you want to change this you can select an item and use the Move buttons on the right hand side. To edit the list, you can add an item to the end of the list or you can use the insert button to add an item between two existing items.

Calculated Values

For some fields you want to be able to calculate a value. One that I frequently use is the Look Ahead Date which calculates a date 14 days (2 weeks) in the future. Click on the **Formula . . .** button and Project brings up the Formula dialog, which here shows the simple formula for the Look Ahead Date.

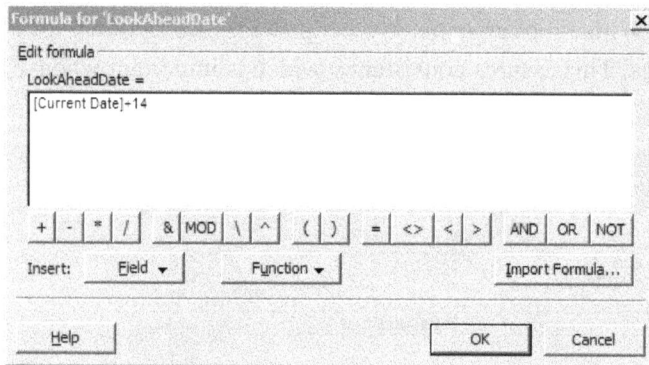

In the dialog area you can see that the Look Ahead Date is calculated by adding 14 to the Current Date. Below the dialog area there is a row of buttons for the most common functions for processing data. Each of these can also be typed in. Below these buttons are a dropdown to access all of the fields that Project maintains and another to access a large number of useful functions. If you know the field name you can type it in square brackets.

A frequently used function is the If function – IIF. For example, with fields like Start, Finish, % Complete and Status Date or Current Date, and nested IIFs, you can create a field to flag tasks that are complete, in-progress, late, etc. You can also display a graphical indicator reflecting that status.

Unfortunately, not all books on Project discuss these functions, but you can just play around with them or go to the Project on-line Help and search on Custom Fields.

Graphical Indicators

The other thing you can do with fields is display the data graphically. The graphics can give you a lot of information about your project schedule with just a glance. One of the text fields I use is Risk Level. I set a value of

Low, Medium or High when the Risk flag is set, or I leave it blank if the task has no assigned risks. For those tasks with risk, the level can be expressed with stop lights – white for Low, yellow for Medium and red for High. These are shown in the dialog box on the next page. (Unfortunately, it's hard to distinguish yellow from white in the black and white figure!)

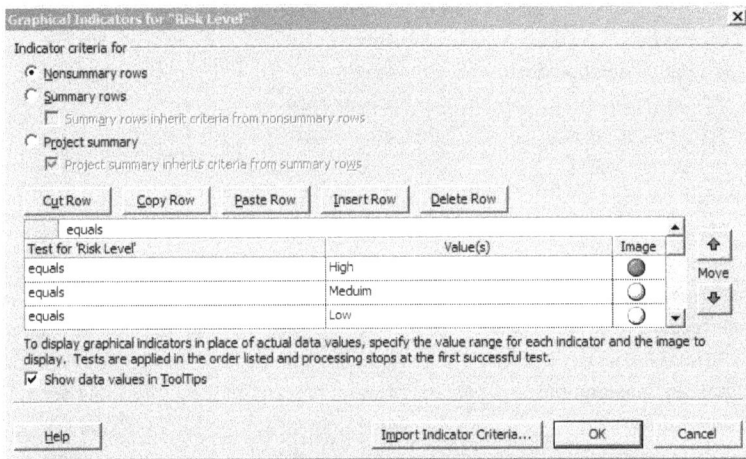

There is a dropdown for the Image with quite a few different shapes, each with a number of colors. We'll see how to take advantage of these when we get to Views.

Filters

With filters you can look at a subset of the tasks in your project. Auto-filter lets you filter on a specific field – e.g. Owner – and custom filters let you filter on multiple fields – e.g. % Complete and Start.

Auto-Filter

With the desired fields filled in, a great feature in Project is the auto-filter. When you have a field in view, with auto filtering you can directly filter on that field. Project provides a dropdown with all possible values and you can choose one. You can also create a custom auto-filter to choose multiple values. The fields I filter on most are Owner and Stage, so these fields are in view in most of my tables. With these I can work on a small subset of tasks as I fill in the duration, predecessors and resources. For example, I might want to focus on Stage 2: Full Data Acquisition. Then, if there are still a lot of tasks, I might also auto-filter to see which of those tasks Joe is responsible for.

Below is a section of the project with the Owner field showing. Note that each title has a drop down arrow indicating that auto-filtering is turned on.

	Task Name ▼	Owner ▼	Resource Names ▼	Work ▼
41	⊟ Data Processing	Amy		504 hrs
42	⊟ Algorithm Design Document	Amy		160 hrs
43	Unit Conversion	Amy	Amy	8 hrs
44	Standard Calculations	Amy	Amy	8 hrs
45	Special Calculations	Amy	Amy	24 hrs
46	Alarm Calculations	Amy	Amy	8 hrs
47	Standard Routines	Amy	Amy	16 hrs
48	Processing Document Release	Amy	Amy	0 hrs
49	Processing Document Review	Amy	Amy,Cliff,Cyndi,Hank	80 hrs
50	Processing Document Update	Amy	Amy	16 hrs
51	Baseline Processing Document	Amy	Amy	0 hrs
52	⊟ Algorithm Development	Amy		344 hrs
53	⊟ Unit Conversion	Amy		32 hrs
54	Temperature Pressure and Flow	Amy	Cyndi	8 hrs
55	Strain	Amy	Cyndi	8 hrs
56	RTD Bridge Completion	Amy	Cyndi	8 hrs
57	Test Unit Conversion	Amy	Cyndi	8 hrs
58	⊟ Standard Calculations	Amy		48 hrs

Clicking on the down arrow for owner shows a list of all of the Owners. Clicking on one of the names will show only those tasks assigned to that name.

	Task Name ▼	Owner ▼	Resource Names ▼	Work ▼
41	⊟ Data Processing	(All)		504 hrs
42	⊟ Algorithm Design Docun	(Custom…)		160 hrs
43	Unit Conversion		Amy	8 hrs
44	Standard Calculations	Amy	Amy	8 hrs
45	Special Calculations	Cliff	Amy	24 hrs
46	Alarm Calculations	Cyndi	Amy	8 hrs
47	Standard Routines	Hank	Amy	16 hrs
48	Processing Document R	Joe	Amy	0 hrs
49	Processing Document Review	Amy	Amy,Cliff,Cyndi,Hank	80 hrs
50	Processing Document Update	Amy	Amy	16 hrs
51	Baseline Processing Document	Amy	Amy	0 hrs

Clicking on **(Custom . . .)** brings up a dialog that allows you to filter on multiple owners. Below it is set up to look at both Joe and Amy, hence the **Or** radio button is checked.

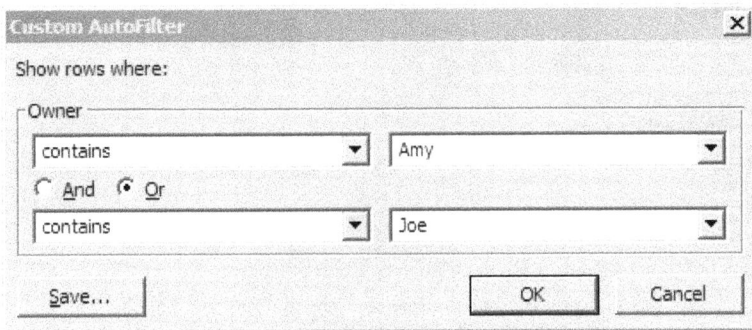

There are quite a few tests other than contains that you can use, but, quite frankly, it's the only one I use when auto-filtering on a custom field.

Although I primarily use Owner, I could also auto-filter on Resource Name. I do this if the Owner field is not in view or when I have resources assigned who do not own the deliverable.

Note, when an element is selected then the column title, in this case Owner, is changed to a bright blue as a reminder that the current schedule has been auto-filtered, and which column has to be reset to All to go back to the entire schedule.

Custom Filters

Auto-filtering is both simple and powerful. I use them most of the time. However, occasionally I want something more complex. To create a custom filter, go to the More Filters dialog:

Version	Menu/Tab	Item	Sub-item
2007	Project	Filtered For	More Filters . . .
2010	View	Filter:	More Filters . . .

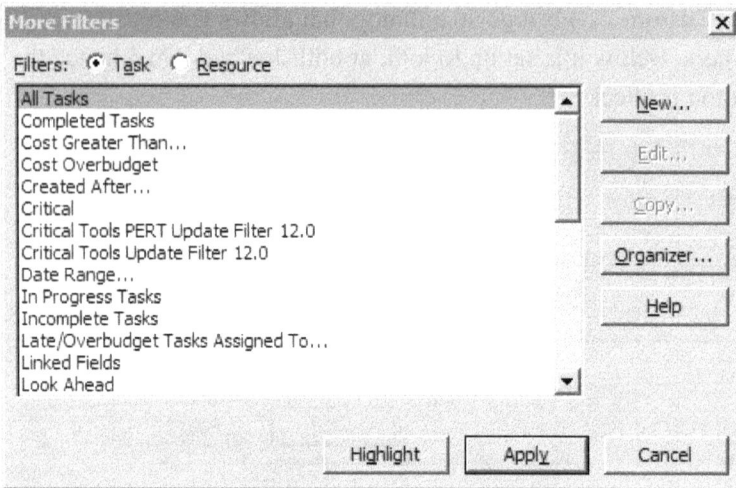

Project has quite a few built in filters, and I highly recommend that you check these out to see what they do and how they are programmed. Date Range is a good one to look at because it uses pop-ups to allow the user to input the dates. Summary and Critical tasks are also interesting because you might like to create a filter to look at only summary or critical tasks that satisfy some other criteria, such as being incomplete or late.

You can use the Date Range filter to do a look ahead to see what people will be doing in the next 2 weeks. However, you have to enter the dates you're interested in via two pop-ups. With the Look Ahead Date, you can automate this. What I am usually interested in is all tasks that are not complete and are scheduled to start within the next two weeks. That is:

% Complete < 100%

And   Start < Look Ahead Date

Click on Look Ahead, which is at the bottom of the list shown, and click on **Edit**. On the next page is the Filter Definition for the Look Ahead filter.

Filter Definition in 'DAS Software'   ×

Name: | Look Ahead | ☑ Show in menu

Filter:

| Cut Row | Copy Row | Paste Row | Insert Row | Delete Row |

And/Or	Field Name	Test	Value(s)
	% Complete	is less than	100%
And	Start	is less than	[LookAheadDate]

☑ Show related summary rows

| Help | | OK | Cancel |

The filter is set up to ignore tasks that are 100% complete, so I am only looking at the active tasks. To create the filter, just click on **New . . .** in the More Filters dialog, type in the name, Look Ahead, and enter the two lines of information shown here.

When I'm creating a schedule, I want to be able to quickly identify those tasks that are missing a predecessor and successor. For this I create a custom Dangling Tasks filter:

Filter Definition in 'DAS Software'   ×

Name: | Dangling Tasks | ☐ Show in menu

Filter:

| Cut Row | Copy Row | Paste Row | Insert Row | Delete Row |

And/Or	Field Name	Test	Value(s)
	Summary	equals	No
And			
	Predecessors	equals	
Or	Successors	equals	

☑ Show related summary rows

| Help | | OK | Cancel |

Note the **And** is on a blank line. This says not to check any summary tasks, and select those regular tasks that either have no predecessor or no successor or both.

Groups

Groups allow you to reorder all of the tasks. I use filters when I am working on the schedule and groups when I want to present it to others.

I can group by Owner, and each owner can clearly see his or her tasks, and they can see the tasks of the other owners. Stage is another field I like to group on. In fact what I usually do is make it a two level group – first stage and then owner. These groups are useful for making a Gantt chart to put up on a wall to show either Owner or both Stages and Owners.

PTo check out the groups Project provides, or to create a custom group, go to the More Groups dialog:

Version	Menu/Tab	Item	Sub-item
2007	Project	Group By:	More Groups . . .
2010	View	Group By	More Groups . . .

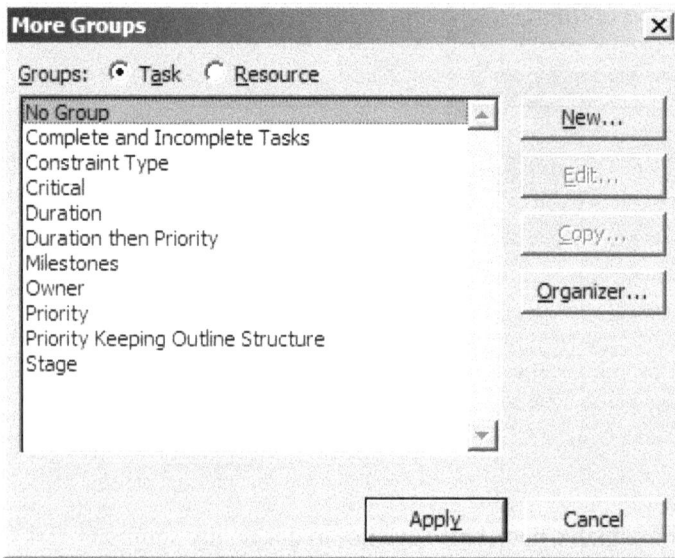

Note that the list contains the custom groups Owner and Stage. When you want to create a custom group, click on the **New . . .** button to bring up the Group Definition dialog. Below is the definition of the Stage group:

This group has two levels: first by Stage and then by Owner: Below is a section of the schedule, filtered for Summary tasks and looking at Stage 1:

Task Name	Duration	Start	Finish
⊟ Stage 1: Basic DAS	49 days	Feb 1 '12	Apr 9 '12
⊟ No Value	3 days	Apr 2 '12	Apr 4 '12
⊟ Stage 1: Basic Data Acqui	3 days	Apr 2 '12	Apr 4 '12
⊟ Amy	22 days	Feb 1 '12	Mar 1 '12
⊟ Interface Design Docume	10 days	Feb 17 '12	Mar 1 '12
⊟ Algorithm Design Docum	12 days	Feb 1 '12	Feb 16 '12
⊟ Cliff	49 days	Feb 1 '12	Apr 9 '12
⊟ Display Design	18 days	Feb 1 '12	Feb 24 '12
⊟ Data Display	31 days	Feb 27 '12	Apr 9 '12
⊟ Joe	43 days	Feb 1 '12	Mar 30 '12
⊟ DAS Design Document	10 days	Feb 1 '12	Feb 14 '12
⊟ DAS Interface Developme	10 days	Mar 2 '12	Mar 15 '12
⊟ Get Raw Data	11 days	Mar 16 '12	Mar 30 '12
⊟ Input Simulator	3 days	Mar 26 '12	Mar 28 '12

Amy, Cliff and Joe each have deliverables to feed into Stage 1. At the top of the Owners is No Value. This is the Integration Stage Summary which has no Owner assigned. It was left without an Owner so it would be on top. Project always puts blank elements on top with No Value.

We'll use this group shortly in a custom strategy view.

Views and Tables

Project maintains a tremendous amount of schedule specific and custom information. Views show you the information you're interested in, using a format that is most useful. The Gantt Chart shows the timeline, the Network Diagram Shows the logic and Resource Usage shows resource allocation over time. Many views, such as the Gantt Chart also have a table of useful tabular data. The power of Project extends to customizing views and tables.

Tables

Project has many tables showing different data that a user might want. For example, the Gantt Chart has the Entry table on the left with the most commonly used parameters to set up a simple schedule. You can easily modify this by adding and deleting columns. There are times however, when you might want to see information that is quite different than the Entry table. Then you can choose to use one of Projects built in tables, modify a Project table, or create a custom table from scratch.

To see the tables Project provides, and to create a custom table, go to the More Tables dialog:

Version	Menu/Tab	Item	Sub-item
2007	View	Table:	More Tables . . .
2010	View	Tables	More Tables . . .

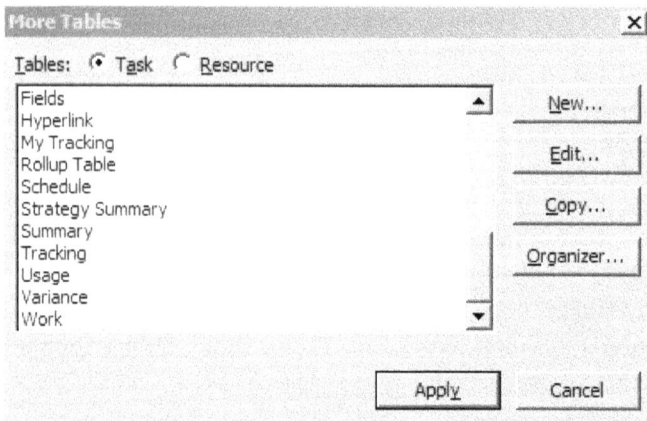

This brings up a list of the currently defined tables. You can select any one and then click on **Edit . . .** to see what parameters are in the table.

There are two custom tables in the list shown: Fields and Strategy Summary. Fields just lists the tasks along with all of the custom fields. This is useful to maintain those fields – that is to change values or add values for new tasks. Strategy Summary is a table we'll use to create a special Strategy view. Selecting it and clicking on **Edit . . .** brings up the Table Definition dialog:

This table only uses the seven parameters listed, but you could add as many as you like. Two of the parameters are custom fields: Risks and Risk Level. Risks has a list of risks from the risk log that apply to a deliverable, and Risk Level is low, medium or high with a graphical indicator. We'll use this table shortly when we create a custom view.

Views

Project also has many different views. To see the list of views and to create a custom view, go to the More Views dialog:

Version	Menu/Tab	Item	Sub-item
2007	View	More Views . . .	
2010	View	More Views	More Views . . .

More Views

Views:
Resource PerCent Usage
Resource Sheet
Resource Usage
Strategy
Task Details Form
Task Entry
Task Form
Task Name Form
Task Sheet
Task Usage
Tracking Gantt

New...
Edit...
Copy...
Organizer...

Apply   Cancel

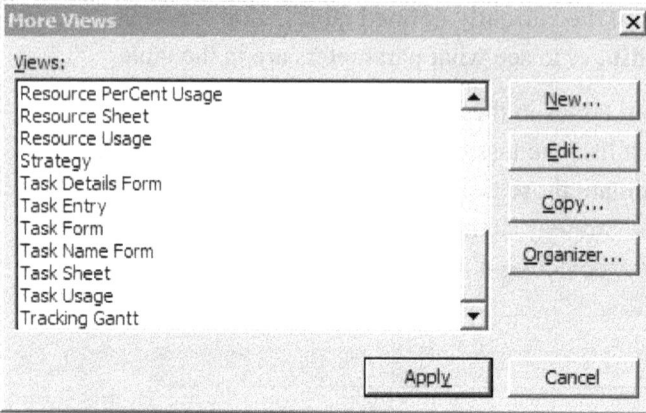

If you haven't already, you should check out the different views. Here we will create a custom view to get a top level view of our strategy. Click on **New ...** This will bring up a pop-up asking if you want a Single View or a Combination View. Since Single View is the default, just click **OK** to bring up the View Definition dialog.

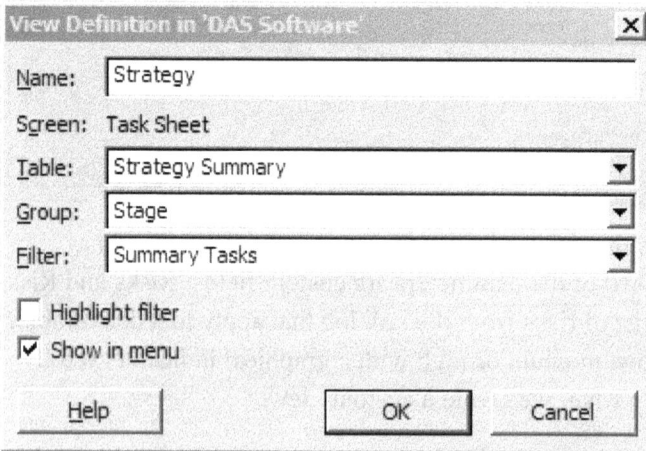

View Definition in 'DAS Software'

Name: Strategy

Screen: Task Sheet

Table: Strategy Summary

Group: Stage

Filter: Summary Tasks

☐ Highlight filter
☑ Show in menu

Help   OK   Cancel

In addition to the Name, the information required includes:

Table   Strategy Summary – the table we just looked at

Group   Stage – the two level Stage and Owner group we created

Filter   Summary Tasks – for this display I want to focus on the deliverables which are the summary tasks

128

The Show in menu box is checked so the view will be available on the View menu in Project 2007 or in the More Views dropdown in 2010.

The resulting display looks like this:

Task Name	Risks	Risk Level	Duration	Start	Finish
⊞ No Value			94 days	Feb 1 '12	Jun 11 '12
⊞ Functional / System Test			72 days	Mar 2 '12	Jun 11 '12
⊞ Stage 1: Basic DAS			49 days	Feb 1 '12	Apr 9 '12
⊞ Stage 2: Full DAS			47 days	Feb 17 '12	Apr 23 '12
⊟ Stage 3: Special Calcs			64 days	Feb 1 '12	Apr 30 '12
⊟ No Value			5 days	Apr 24 '12	Apr 30 '12
⊟ Stage 3: Special Data Calculation			5 days	Apr 24 '12	Apr 30 '12
⊟ Amy			20 days	Mar 12 '12	Apr 6 '12
⊟ Special Calculations	3,9	🔵	15 days	Mar 12 '12	Mar 30 '12
⊟ Alarm Calculations			5 days	Apr 2 '12	Apr 6 '12
⊟ Cliff			9 days	Mar 9 '12	Mar 21 '12
⊟ Display: System Diagnostic			3 days	Mar 9 '12	Mar 13 '12
⊟ Display: Decision Trees	4,8	⚪	6 days	Mar 14 '12	Mar 21 '12
⊟ Cyndi			28 days	Feb 1 '12	Mar 9 '12
⊟ Archive: Design Document			6 days	Feb 1 '12	Feb 8 '12
⊟ Archive: Current Data			7 days	Mar 1 '12	Mar 9 '12

This view provides a top level summary of the stages in the project, who is involved in each stage, and what deliverables are they responsible for. The key to a view like this is making sure that Owner and Stage are properly filled out for all tasks and summary tasks.

Here I'm interested in Stage 3, so Functional/System Test, Stage 1 and Stage 2 are closed up. At the top of Stage 3 is the No Value. That is the Stage 3 summary task has no resource assigned. As I pointed out, by leaving Owner blank it will be on the top of the list by itself. You can see it is supposed to start on April 24 and finish on April 30.

The graphical indicators highlight the risks associated with both Special Calculations and Decision Trees. The Special Calculations are a high risk, so this is something you would track closely to proactively manage the risks as you're managing the schedule.

With a few custom fields and a custom table, you can create a useful, high level view of your project. You can add fields to the table, such as % Complete, Start Variance or an Earned Value parameter such as SPI, to see even more about the status of each integration stage. You're only limited by your understanding of Project and your imagination.

Resource Percent Usage View

I rely on the Resource Usage View when creating my schedule, but I prefer to see % Allocation rather than Work. I generally set the timescale to months and hours per month can vary since the number of workdays, holidays and vacation days vary. So it's hard to tell at a glance what a number means even though Project highlights overallocations in red. % Allocation is based on available work time and is much easier to interpret. Below is a portion of a Resource Usage showing % Allocation:

Resource Name	Work	Details	Qtr 1, 2012			Qtr 2, 2012		
			Jan	Feb	Mar	Apr	May	Jun
⊞ Joe	520 hrs	% Alloc.		81%	95%	114%	13%	
⊞ Amy	512 hrs	% Alloc.		124%	100%	76%		
⊞ Cyndi	424 hrs	% Alloc.		110%	100%	38%		
⊞ Cliff	512 hrs	% Alloc.		133%	100%	43%	22%	
⊞ Hank	600 hrs	% Alloc.		43%	95%	71%	100%	33%

Here you can readily spot which resources are overallocated, which are critical – at or near 100% through most of the project – and which have time to help out the overloaded or critical resources.

I create a separate Resource Percent Usage view so I can also look at hours when necessary. To do this:

- In the More Views Dialog select Resource Usage and click **Copy**
- In the View Definition dialog, change the Name to Resource Percent Usage and click **OK**.
- Click **Apply** to bring up the Resource Percent Usage Display
- On the right hand side, where the detail hours are shown, right click and select Detail Styles on the pop-up
- This brings up the Detail Styles Dialog (opposite page)
  The Available Fields list is scrolled to the bottom and Percent Allocation is near the top of the fields that are shown
- With Work Selected in the Show these fields box, click **Hide**
- Select Percent Allocation and click **Show**
- Click **OK**

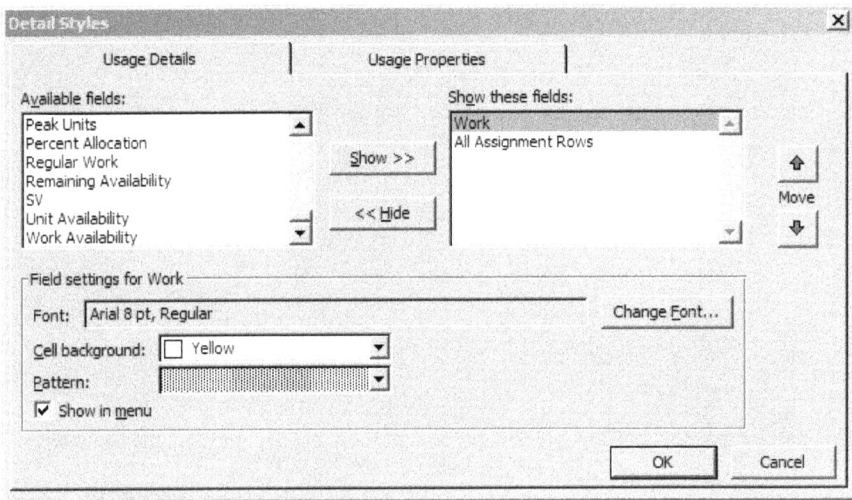

Now you have a more intuitive view to quickly assess how evenly the work is allocated to your assigned resources.

With discipline, an iterative process highlighting concurrent risk analysis and a powerful planning tool like Microsoft Project to pull it all together, you can make a difference as a project manager!

www.ingramcontent.com/pod-product-compliance
Lightning Source LLC
Chambersburg PA
CBHW070406200326
41518CB00011B/2079